The first prototype of the Ta 154 returns to the ramp after a test flight.

Tank Ta 154

by Manfred Griehl

Until the beginning of 1942 the heavy bombers of Royal Air Force Bomber Command only appeared in the night skies over Germany in relatively small numbers. The air war situation did not change drastically until the 1,000 bomber attack on the cathedral city of Cologne on 30 May 1942 and the subsequent heavy raids on Essen and Bremen. In addition, the De Havilland Mosquito, the so-called "wooden wonder," was operating by night in ever growing numbers. Its outstanding performance allowed it to carry out its missions with unbelievable speed and unprecedented precision.

During a conference held on 18 August 1942 by the Minister of Air Armaments, *Generalfeldmarschall* Erhard Milch, possible uses were sought for the Jumo 211 inline engine, which was now available in quantity. During a development conference less than one month later, on 11 September 1942, the use of "homogenous wood" as a construction material for airframes was judged to be "very promising," and its further development was assigned a high priority. At the same time, on 16 September 1942 GFM Milch spoke out in favor of a light, high-speed night bomber. The wooden construction method had much in its favor in view of the materials situation, but the development risk could not be overlooked.

On 17 September 1942 GFM Milch stated: "...the planned night bomber will not be available so quickly!" Since the German aviation industry was in no position to produce long-range, four-engined heavy bombers, soon afterwards Focke-Wulf submitted a proposal for a counterpart to the D.H. Mosquito, an unarmed, twin-engined, high-speed bomber ("Design 1"), for the RLM's consideration. The proposed aircraft was of mixed construction with Jumo 211 F inline engines. Professor Kurt Tank took charge of the project personally. *Oberingenieur* Ludwig Mittelhuber was responsible for design. In charge of construction was *Oberingenieur* Ernst Nipp. *Oberin-genieur* Gotthold Mathias was responsible for handling characteristics, while *Dipl.-Ing.* Herbert Wolf was responsible for performance.

According to the proposal, the innovative machine was to be 50% wood and 39% steel. The remaining 11% would consist of other materials, such as fabric covering or so-called "Heine-Platten" (Heine Plates) 5 to 8 mm thick. Of the wooden components, more than half were of beech plywood in thicknesses of 0.8 to 6 mm, solid pine and pressed beechwood.

The machine was designed as a shoulder-wing aircraft with retractable undercarriage and was to be fitted with a two-tank GM 1 system for increased performance. Fuel capacity was 1,400 kg in three self-sealing SG tanks.

In its first proposal of 22 September 1942, the company assumed that the high-speed bomber would be produced without defensive armament.

At the end of September Milch requested a reworked design incorporating defensive armament. "Design 1" for a single-seat machine was subsequently reworked by 7 October 1942. The new bomber was to be armed with two rearward-firing MG 151 cannon. It was to be capable of carrying a maximum bomb load of one SC 1000 or two SC 500s. Furthermore, it could carry a Type F5 bomb dispenser with 223 SD 2 or 42 SC 10 bombs. Also possible was the installation of eight AB 36 or 42 bomb dispensers. The unarmored machine's aiming system consisted of a BZA 20 bombsight. Radio equipment of production aircraft was to consist of a FuG 16Z with Diekmann DF set plus a FuG 25 IFF set.

Artist's concept of the planned Ta 211 two-seater.

On 9 October 1942 full responsibility for the development of the new bomber was transferred to Kurt Tank. The growing weight of Allied air attacks probably led the *Technische Amt* to abandon further work on this development, the later Ta 211, and instead concentrate on bolstering Germany's own defensive capabilities. A few days later, on 16 October 1942, the *Generalfeldmarschall* decided to place more emphasis on the secondary role of "night fighter." With its long endurance, the second design of the Ta 211 seemed eminently suitable. The second version of the Ta 211 proposed to the *Technische Amt* (TA) likewise dated from 22 September 1942 and unlike the high-speed bomber was a two-seater. Its crew consisted of a pilot and radio-operator/observer. In keeping with the night fighter role, the machine's radio equipment was more extensive. This consisted of a FuG 212 search radar, whose mast-type antennas were to be mounted in the nose of the aircraft, plus

Mock-up of the Ta 154 night fighter with FuG 202 airborne radar.

a FuG 17, PeilG VI direction-finding set, a FuBl 2F, a FuG 101 precision altimeter, the FuG 25 IFF set and a FuG 28a. Fixed armament was to consist of two MK 103 and two MK 151 cannon, all installed in the fuselage. Fuel capacity was 1,850 liters contained in several self-sealing tanks in the fuselage.

Designs 1 and 2 of the future Ta 211 still had the then typical tailwheel. "Design 3" of 14 October 1942 was based on the two preceding designs but for the first time included a tricycle undercarriage. Equipment and electronics were essentially similar to the previous design, however, armament had been bolstered through the addition of one obliquely-mounted MK 108 with 150 rounds of ammunition.

One factor boded well for the introduction of the Ta 211 with its relatively higher performance: even though the current generation of night fighters, the Bf 110 and Ju 88, was achieving considerable success as a result of improved radar and refined control methods, they lacked the development potential required to allow them to keep pace with enemy developments. Also, shortages of raw materials were becoming increasingly serious.

Since Kurt Tank's design was constructed largely of plywood and its projected performance figures had caught the eye of the *Technische Amt*, it seemed that a capable second generation night fighter had been found.

Wind tunnel model of the Ta 154 with Jumo 211 F/N inline engines.

In mid-October Erhard Milch decided to set aside the former high-speed bomber studies and to concentrate on the night and bad weather fighter equipped with Jumo 211 engines. Consequently, a preliminary contract was issued to Focke-Wulf for fifty machines and assigned the DE level of priority. On 20 October 1942 *Reichsmarschall* Göring also gave his approval. Taking into consideration the previous proposals, a "Type Description Night Fighter Ta 211" was created by 23 October 1942 and subsequently submitted to the RLM in Berlin.

On 30 October 1942 GFM Milch decreed that the assembly and testing of the first prototype Ta 211 was to be carried out as quickly as possible in Langenhagen near Hanover, since the

Wunstorf and Detmold locations were considered unsuitable. On 13 November 1942 the *Technische Amt* gave its approval for the former "Focke-Wulf Night Fighter" project, which was known internally as the Ta 211, to continue, but now under the designation Ta 154. At the same time Focke-Wulf was instructed to build ten prototypes, the Ta 154 V1 to V10. On 8 January 1943 a "Ta 154 Start-up Conference" was held in Berlin. It was there that the first problems came to light. The most serious of these was a shortage of personnel qualified to work with wood. It was predicted that the Jumo 211 would provide insufficient power to keep pace with enemy developments, however, the Jumo 213 was only then being bench run and was not yet ready for service use. Erhard Milch, who saw the Ta 154 and Bf 110 G as stopgap solutions pending availability of the He 219, changed the focus of the machine's development.

According to the wishes of the *Technische Amt*, the machine was to be outfitted with an armament of four MK 103 cannon. An installation investigation was begun in March 1943, but the results were negative. In June 1943 a request was received from the *General der Jagdflieger* that all Ta 154s be equipped with GM 1. On the other hand, the *General der Kampfflieger* called for a bomb bay and the use of the Ta 154 as a command aircraft. To the *General der Aufklärungsflieger* the Ta 154 and the Do 335 were ideal reconnaissance aircraft.

On 18 June 1943 it was decided to concentrate production in three areas, involving numerous subcontractors, and so dislocate it that it would be relatively invulnerable to air attack. The production areas were to manufacture the following variants in large quantities:

- Production Area Silesia: A-2, B-1 and C-1
- Production Area Thuringia: A-1, A-2, B-1, B-2 and C-4
- Production Area Warthe District: A-1, A-2, B-1, B-2 and C-4.

The first problem, so it was rashly assumed, would be the provision of suitably powerful inline engines like the Jumo 213. The Jumo 211 power plant then available had by now proved inadequate, since the early flame dampers on both sides of the engine and the antenna array of the FuG 212 radar resulted in a loss of airspeed of between 35 and 40 kph.

Cockpit mock-up of the Ta 154 two-seat night fighter.

Radio operator's position in the mock-up.

The Ta 154 V1 on the company airfield at Langenhagen.

This was demonstrated during flight testing of the Ta 154 V1 in July 1943, but even more so after the first flights by the Ta 154 V3, which was equipped with the FuG 212 C-1. As a result there were renewed calls for the installation of GM-1 (glycol-methanol) injection. However, on 18 August 1943 calculations showed that the performance of the Ta 154 equipped with Jumo 211 F engines and GM 1 would still be inadequate. Furthermore, demands by the *Technische Amt* for drop tanks to increase range, greater fuel capacity and oblique armament were becoming loud. These changes would result in a further drop in the Ta 154's performance. On 12 October 1943 the *E-Stelle Rechlin* gave its detailed opinion on the calculated performance of the Ta 154 and expressed doubts as to the performance figures claimed by the manufacturer. Estimated speed with combat power at maximum boost altitude was barely 580 kph instead of the 615 kph claimed by Focke-Wulf. Service ceiling was only 9,400 meters instead of 10,400 meters. All remaining values were estimated to be somewhat lower than those cited by Focke-Wulf. In all, performance figures were approximately 5% below those claimed by the manufacturer.

For this reason Focke-Wulf made increasingly urgent demands for rapid delivery of Jumo 213 engines, however, these were not to be available for fighter use until the summer of 1944. As a result, subsequent testing had to be done with the sufficiently proven Jumo 211 F of N engines.

On 29 October 1943 *Hauptmann* Thierfelder test flew the Ta 154 and gave the machine a "thoroughly positive assessment," apart from what he felt were excessively high control forces. During trials, however, there were numerous problems with the undercarriage, flaps, and cooling system. All of this resulted in delays, in some cases lasting months, until 1944.

On 3 December 1943 the B model of the Ta 154 was canceled, and the *Technische Amt* ordered the introduction of the new Ta 154 C standard variant with a metal nose and Jumo 213 power plants. In the meantime, the Ta 154's technical problems were becoming more acute. The development conference of 17 March 1944 characterized production to date as a debacle, mainly due to unsatisfactory gluing and the lack of sufficient trained personnel. In addition, it had become clear that delays in Jumo production were going to be more serious than originally thought. Consequently, the first production aircraft could not be expected before March 1944.

Further criticism came from *Oberst* Diesing, head of planning in the RLM, who together with GFM Milch complained to Kurt Tank about the Ta 154's poor flight characteristics. According to the *Oberst*, a "normal pilot" would have difficulty mastering the new machine.

The Ta 154 V1 prior to installation of flame dampers.

He also declared that airframe vibration and the loss of fuselage components when the guns were fired were unlikely to increase confidence in the Ta 154. Kurt Tank subsequently promised to develop a new and improved tail section in order to improve the machine's handling characteristics.

Oberstleutnant Kneemeyer was also unsettled. After flying the Ta 154 V5 he feared a repetition of the Me 210 disaster. Resignedly, *Generalfeldmarschall* Milch was forced to admit that the hoped-for copy of the D.H. Mosquito was an impossibility because the necessary glues were still not available. At the end of March Hermann Göring came out in favor of the development and criticized the *Generalfeldmarschall* for "neglecting the vital Ta 154 fighter."

On 12 April 1944 Flugkapitän Hans Sander demonstrated a prototype before the R*eichsmarschall* at Rechlin, which of course only strengthened his existing view of the aircraft.

On 24 April 1944 the aircraft construction program for the Focke-Wulf prototypes called for nine prototypes of wooden construction with metal elevators, rudder, and flaps. Of these aircraft (WerkNr. 00001 to 00009, later 100001 to 100009) the V3 had already crashed at Sorau on 29 February 1944, while the V4 was under repair as a result of a crash.

Almost all of these prototypes and pre-production series aircraft were still equipped with the inadequate Jumo 211 in the summer of 1944, however. Factory trials at Langenhagen soon revealed additional weak points in the design. The undercarriage and hydraulics in particular were prone to failure.

A detailed report issued by the Focke-Wulf company on 20 May 1944 examined the crashes that had occurred so far: the first crash landing involving the Ta 154 V1 on 31 July 1943 was the result of an excessive sink rate on landing. As a result, both of the main landing gear's struts had collapsed. This led to several attempts to redesign the undercarriage to bear 20% greater longitudinal force.

On 18 February 1944 the Ta 154 V4 was involved in a crash landing when both main undercarriage elements retracted involuntarily when the aircraft touched down. The error was probably in the aircraft's electrics and it did not result in any modifications. A few days later, on 28 February 1944, the nosewheel of the Ta 154 V3 collapsed, resulting in the destruction of the wooden forward fuselage. The pilot, the only crewman in the prototype, sustained minor injuries. The aircraft's nosewheel had a castor of only 9%. As a result, it was decided that the nosewheels of later machines, especially the first production examples, should have a castor of 23%. This problem had

Prof. Kurt Tank climbs into the cockpit of a Ta 154.

Tank is briefed on the Ta 154 V1's instrumentation.

Kurt Tank test flies the Ta 154 V1 at Langenhagen on 7/07/1943.

The Ta 154 V1 taxies for takeoff.

Prof. Kurt Tank at the controls of his Ta 154.

angles to the direction of landing in falling terrain, a total write-off. A double piston rod failure in one of the aircraft's Jumo 211's resulted in a fire, and the subsequent forced landing went awry. The wooden cockpit area was totally destroyed. Had the fuselage been made of metal it is highly probable that the crew would have survived. The accident probably convinced all involved to introduce a metal fuselage as soon as possible and to proceed with the Ta 154 C series. This would have mini-

not been foreseen because nosewheel undercarriages were still the exception in the German aviation industry at that time.

On 7 April 1944 one of the main undercarriage legs of the Ta 154 V5 failed. The pilot subsequently landed the machine on the remaining undercarriage leg and nosewheel, the airframe sustaining only minor damage as a result. One engine gondola was slightly dented, and the blades of one propeller were broken off. This failure was due to a material problem, as a bolt in the retraction mechanism had broken under a load factor of just 1.5. On 18 April 1944 a test flight by the Ta 154 V9 ended in the total destruction of the aircraft. The machine rolled sharply to the right when the flaps were lowered and the right wingtip and horizontal stabilizer contacted the ground. H. Meyer was killed, while the pilot escaped with injuries. The Ta 154's landing flaps were standard split, variable-camber flaps, and both ailerons were supposed to extend when the flaps were lowered. In several previous cases one dropped aileron had been observed, leading to a design change affecting all prototypes and production aircraft to prevent a similar recurrence.

Another Ta 154 was damaged on 18 April 1944 when a jammed nosewheel door prevented the nosewheel undercarriage from extending. A request was made for a "landing skid" beneath the nose and fuselage center section in order to prevent further damage to the prototypes from nosewheel-related accidents which might delay tactical testing.

Soon afterwards, on 6 May 1944, a landing by the Ta 154 V8 also ended in a catastrophe. The crew of Otto and Rettig were killed in the accident near Goslar, while the aircraft lay at right

Prof. Kurt Tank leaving the cockpit of the first prototype.

The Ta 154 V1 (WerkNr. 100001) later bore the radio call sign TE+FE.

Engine test run at Langenhagen; in the foreground the four flame dampers.

mized or even eliminated the problems that occurred during static firing trials at Langenhagen, in which sections of the fuselage skinning were damaged.

At this time the RLM also finalized the armament of future Ta 154 variants. The Ta 154 A-2 and A-4 were both to be equipped with two MG 151/20 and two MK 108 cannon. Night fighters would also have two obliquely-mounted MK 108 cannon in the rear fuselage. On the other hand, those Ta 154s which were to be used in the day *Zerstörer* role were to be equipped with two MK 103 and two MG 151/15 cannon. All of the other armament proposals submitted by the manufacturer were dropped for reasons of standardization. The same applied to the installation of a BK 5 to the left of the pilot. The airframe lacked the necessary structural strength for the installation of the heavy cannon.

New problems arose in the area of armaments at the end of 1944, however, as the mounts proved insufficiently strong to absorb the recoil of the automatic weapons. This resulted in a redesign. Those aircraft that saw action, provided they did not have a metal fuselage, had to be employed over northern Germany with a reduced armament of two MG 151s. In addition to improving the undercarriage and the forward fuselage including armament package, the wooden wings continued to attract a great deal of attention. The search for the ideal bonding material for the wooden Ta 154 A proved extremely time consuming. It was thought that a usable solution had finally been found in "Tego-Film," however the destruction of the manufacturing firm caused considerable problems. Focke-Wulf had to turn to other manufacturers who lacked the appropriate know-how. In spite of all efforts, the problems of glue production had still not been solved by the end of May 1944, as Professor Tank was forced to admit during a conference. From the beginning, additional prototypes had been planned for the purpose of testing the structural strength of the mixed-construction Ta 154. In addition to the V1a design mock-up, the program called for the Ta 154 V11 to V14a and the V24. The V14 and V14a were earmarked for static testing of the projected C-series.

The beginning of the end of the Ta 154 showed itself in a meeting between Göring, Milch, Galland, Heinkel, Tank, Vogt, Frydag, and Saur on the Obersalzberg on 25 May 1944. *Reichsmarschall* Göring turned to Professor Tank: "The machine is supposed to be in the program now, but I find that it is not. As well the adhesive situation is still unsatisfactory and performance is far below what was projected."

Kurt Tank was unable to provide adequate justification for the stagnation of Ta 154 development. Only in the area of the adhesive question was he able to refer to the "Polystal" glue, which made it possible to satisfactorily bond the wooden components. When questioned by Hermann Göring, *Oberst* Edgar Petersen, the commander of test stations (KdE), replied that he was unable to give an assessment of the machine since all of the prototypes were still with Focke-Wulf, where testing was limited. Furthermore, the *General der Jagdflieger*, *Generalmajor* Galland, declared that the Ta 154's handling qualities still left something to be desired and that the machine's engine-out performance could not meet the requirements of the front-line units. The *Generalmajor* stated that he did not expect any major improvement in the aircraft's handling characteristics even if more powerful engines, like the Jumo 213, were used. In his view, the aircraft's wooden construction made even a belly landing a serious risk for the crews, whereupon Kurt Tank immediately demanded an aluminum cockpit for the Ta 154. The continuation of Ta 154 development, especially series

The first flight of the Ta 154 was made by *Flugkapitän* Hans Sander.

Handling trials were carried out at Langenhagen at the end of July 1943.

Rear view of the Ta 154 V1.

production, was thus on the razor's edge.

From May of 1944 the western Allies obviously became aware of the threat that a successful Ta 154 might pose to their bomber fleets. Langenhagen was the target of a strafing attack. On 29 May 1944 Allied bombs fell on the factory in Posen, and the glue manufacturer, the Goldschmitt Company ("Tegofilm"). But even without the intervention of the RAF, interest in the Ta 154's development on the part of the *Technische Amt* and the fighter staff was waning. On 17 June 1944 the delivery plans established by the fighter staff no longer included the Ta 154. On 3 July *Oberst* Petersen again called attention to the Ta 154's undercarriage situation and the adhesive problem. But this was probably no longer of any consequence. Three days later *Generalfeldmarschall* Milch announced: "We have therefore decided to strike the Ta 154 and 254 completely; the *Reichsmarschall* and the *Führer* have already authorized this."

On 2 August 1944, therefore, *Generalfeldmarschall* Milch issued the following order: "Completed aircraft (154) are to be sidelined, major components must not be completed. It is forbidden to use even one more drop of gasoline for the 154! I make express reference to the regulations concerning sabotage!" The chief of staff of the fighter staff and representative of Reichsminister Speer, *Hauptdienstleiter* Karl-Otto Saur, added the following on 6 August 1944: "The suggestion that the Ta 154 is still needed in the interests of the company is out of the question!"

On 14 August 1944 the OKL General Staff forbade Focke-Wulf to undertake any new construction or repair of the Ta 154. The 22 aircraft under production were to become property of the

Front view of the Ta 154 V1.

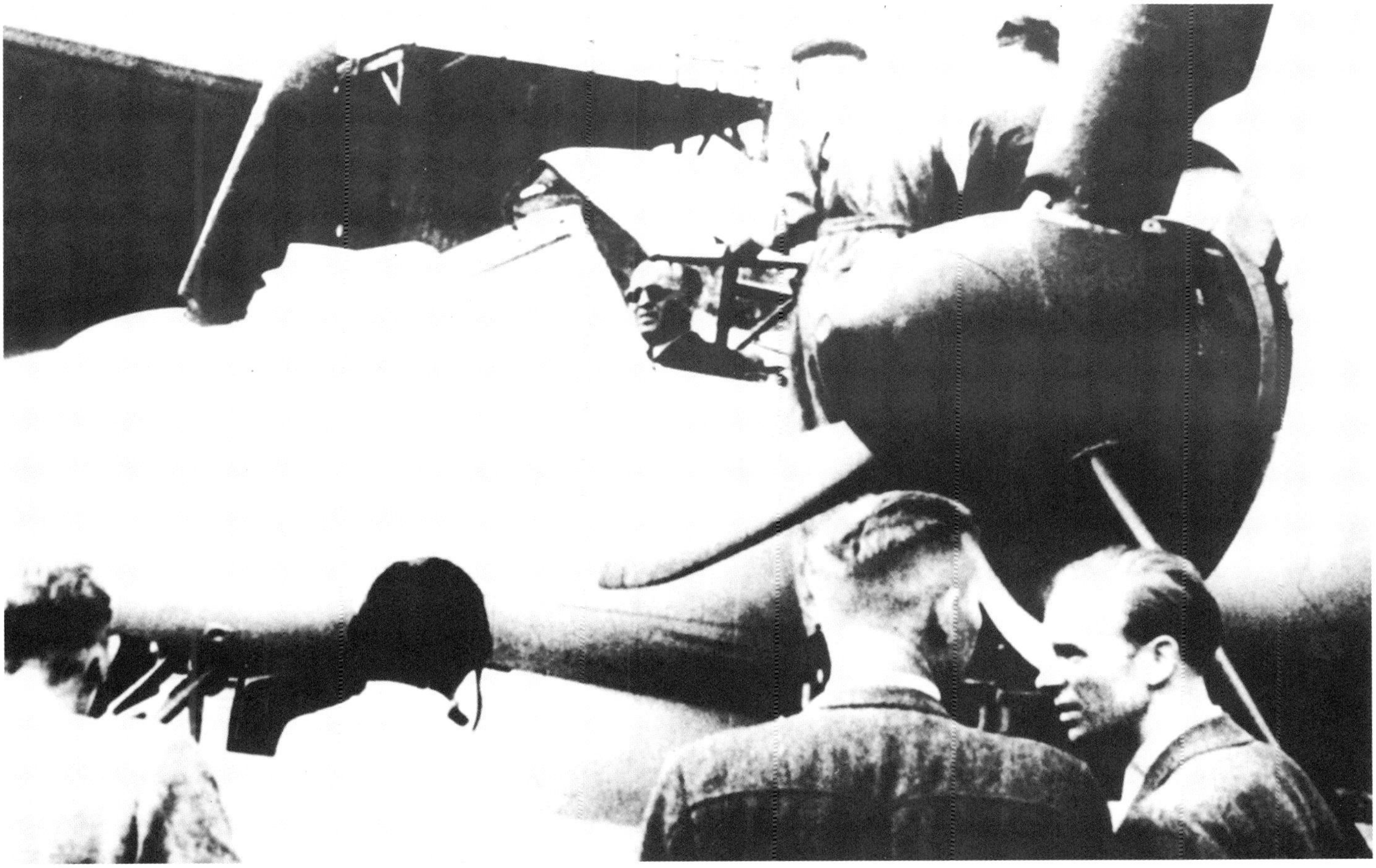

Pre-flight conversation. In the cockpit is Flugbaumeister Hans Sander.

Reich immediately. This was bolstered by a teletype message on 21 August, according to which all machines were to be handed over to the Quartermaster-General. Production of new Ta 154s, at least, had met its end.

In September and October 1944 work continued on several more machines at the Erfurt assembly plant on the authorization of HDL Sauer. On 7 November 1944, however, the *General der Jagdflieger* ruled that these aircraft would not be accepted by the *Luftwaffe*. In spite of the war situation, testing of the Ta 154 resumed in autumn 1944. Last flights were made by the *Stab* of III/NJG 3 in April 1945.

Factory Trials

Production of the first prototypes began in spring 1943. After initial deliveries in December 1942, the West German plywood manufacturer Hugo Bresser and Co. received an order for 89,248 cubic meters of plywood. Further contracts were issued to the firm of Brüning and Son in Lüneburg. The order covered wood for fifty prototype aircraft and more than 330 production machines.

Construction of the fist prototypes took longer than planned because of problems in bonding wood and steel components. At the same time performance estimates were made for the pre-production series (A-0), which was to be equipped with a FuG 212a radar system. Meanwhile, work continued at a high tempo on completion of the first prototype with Jumo 211 F engines and nosewheel undercarriage.

The first prototype of the Ta 154, the V1 (WerkNr. 100001, TE + FE), made its maiden flight at Langenhagen on 1 July 1943. At the controls was *Flugkapitän* Hans Sander. Kurt Tank test flew the machine, which was still unarmed and equipped with provisional radio equipment, on 1 July 1943. Beginning on 21 July the machine's Jumo 211 F engines were exchanged for Jumo 211 Ns. The aircraft was not fitted with flame dampers or fixed armament. The FuG 212 was to be fitted to later prototypes since the V1 was mainly intended for factory performance trials. Canopy jettisoning trials took place at Langenhagen on 23 July with representatives of the *E-Stelle Rechlin* taking part. Soon afterwards, on 28 July, Beauvais and Böttcher, both of the *E-Stelle Rechlin*, test flew the Ta 154 V1 at Langenhagen.

Three days later, during its 47th flight, the aircraft sustained considerable damage in a failed landing; repairs lasted almost a month. The aircraft was flown until 5 August 1944 and was subsequently lost in the destructive air raid on Langenhagen. The second prototype, the Ta 154 V2 (WerkNr. 100002,

Ta 154 mock-up with the antenna array for the Lichtenstein C-1 radar.

Proof loading test on a Ta 154 airframe (probably the Ta 154 V2).

TE + FF), was completed at the end of August 1943 and at the beginning of September was closely examined by representatives of the *Technische Amt* and *E-Stelle Rechlin* at Langenhagen.

As well, an inspection of the 1:1 mock-up with Lichtenstein SN-2 system, which was supposed to replace the FuG 212 C-1 originally planned for the production aircraft, took place in Bad Eilsen. This mainly involved officers of the E-*Stelle Werneuchen* and the *Technische Amt*. The Ta 154 V2 flew for the first time on 10 September 1943, and apart from endurance trials was mainly used for tests with various types of flame damper and for testing the cooling system.

The aircraft was later retrofitted with a FuG 212 C-1 radar, a nosewheel with greater castor, and a dorsal gun position with a MG 81 Z. Like the V1, the two Jumo 211 Fs were replaced with Jumo 211 N power plants. The prototype was completely destroyed in an air raid on Langenhagen on 5 August 1944.

The Ta 154 V3 took to the air for the first time on 25 November 1943 under the command of company pilot Werner Bartsch, and on 10 January 1944 went to the *E-Stelle Rechlin* for a brief period.

The aircraft was damaged in a forced landing at Sorau and was later lost in the air raid on Langenhagen. The third prototype was the second aircraft equipped as a night fighter with a FuG 212 C-1 (later C-2) airborne radar and four MG 151/20 cannon. The machine was equipped with flame dampers and Jumo 211 N power plants driving VS 11 propellers.

The first flight by the Ta 154 V4 took place on 19 January 1944. The flight by factory pilot Werner Bartsch and his observer Herr Schorn, lasted just eight minutes (10:56 to 11:04 AM).

The aircraft had a fixed armament of two MK 108 and two MG 151 cannon. On 12 and 13 February the machine was tested with two 300-liter drop tanks. Other test objectives included determining the aircraft's maximum speed at various power settings (Jumo 211 F), endurance tests of the radiators, functioning of the landing flaps and range of visibility using periscopes. By 18 February 1944 the V4 had logged a total of 37 hours, 18 minutes flying time in 36 flights. The majority of the flights were made by the extremely experienced company pilots Sander, Bartsch, Mondry, and Carl. After the trials the head of the testing department, Fl*ugkapitän* Sander, discovered cracks in the propeller blades. The carriage of two underwing drop tanks resulted in a loss of airspeed of just 20 kph, while the tanks had virtually no effect on handling.

On 25 February 1942 at Langenhagen, Werner Bartsch took the fifth prototype (WerkNr. 100005, TE + FI) up on its maiden flight. On 10 March the machine went to Tarnewitz for weapons testing, and on 7 April its undercarriage was damaged in an accident. What became of the machine after September 1944 is not known. The V5 was one of the prototypes which was re-engined with Jumo 213 A power plants driving VS 111 propellers in place of the Jumo 211 N. The change of engines resulted in a shift in the aircraft's cg, consequently the main undercarriage was moved back 0.16 m.

The Ta 154 V3 parked at Langenhagen.

The Ta 154 V6 made its first flight on 18 March 1943, and between 10 June and 22 September 1944 was tested at Rechlin. At the end of September the machine was equipped with two Jumo 213 A engines driving VS 111 propellers. The prototype was fitted with a nosewheel with a greater castor range and a K12 autopilot. In October the machine, which was used mainly for trials with the electronics, was assigned to the *Luftwaffe* to train Ta 154 crews.

The Ta 154 V7 completed its first flight on 25 March 1944 and on 9 April was damaged by enemy action. The machine still had the old-style nosewheel and Jumo 211 N engines. On 5 August 1944 this prototype was also destroyed at Langenhagen by Allied bombing.

The Ta 154 V8 served as a prototype with two Jumo 213 A-1 engines and had propeller blades made of so-called cross-wood. The nosewheel was of the later, wide-castor type. The machine had a small horizontal stabilizer and rudder and was neither armed nor equipped with an antenna array for any kind of airborne radar. The aircraft was test flown on 8 April and 3 May 1944 by Hans Sander, accompanied by Herr Schorn. On 5 May the crew of Otto and Schorn carried out the aircraft's fourth test flight. Prior to this 250 kg of ballast had been added and the heating system had been declared serviceable. The purpose of the tragic fifth flight was to determine the aircraft's performance with Jumo 213 A engines, which was to result in an engine fire.

Side view of the Ta 154 V3, WerkNr. 100003.

The Ta 154 V9 (WerkNr. 100009, TE + FM) was intended as a prototype for familiarizing new pilots. The machine, which was probably assembled in Posen, was lost on its maiden flight on 18 April 1944. The V9 crashed on landing at Erfurt, in which company test pilot Bartsch was injured and his observer, Hans Meyer, was killed. The tenth prototype, the Ta 154 V10 (WerkNr. 100010, TE + FN), was completed in Langenhagen in May 1944 and from there carried out its successful maiden flight on 4 June. The aircraft was equipped with two Jumo 213 A-1 engines driving VS 9 propellers and was used in the factory trials program at Langenhagen.

The next three prototypes, the Ta 154 V11 to V13 (WerkNr. 100011 to 100013) were produced as A-0s in Erfurt in the summer of 1944 and were used in various structural tests for the different Ta 154 A variants.

The Variants

In spring 1944 the Ta 154 variants A through D were in the advanced planning stage. The all-wood Ta 154 A was to be produced as a day fighter (A-1, A-1/R1 and A-2), night fighter (A-4) and training aircraft with dual controls (A-3). The selected power plants were either the Jumo 211 N or R. In the end the *Luftwaffe* received only a handful of operational A-1s, A-2s and A-4s as a result of a modification program.

Development of the Ta 154 B was canceled at the end of May 1944, since the cost of the changes was too great. The Ta 154 C powered by Jumo 213 engines was supposed to replace the Ta 154 A variants as soon as possible and was conceived in three differently-equipped versions. Plans called for a two-seat night fighter (C-1), a single-seat day fighter and day fighter-bomber (C-2), and a two-seat day fighter (C-3) which was otherwise similar to the C-2.

The last planned version, the Ta 154 D, became the basic model of the later Ta 254 design, which was supposed to go into production in two versions (A-1 and A-2) in 1945.

Undercarriage function check on the Ta 154 V3; the V3 was equipped with a rearwards-firing defensive position.

Production

The widely-dispersed, large-scale production of the Ta 154 never got beyond the starting point because of the war situation and numerous problems associated with building the wooden aircraft.

In the field of wood construction there was a shortage of trained engineers, foremen, and skilled workers. As well the jigs for the construction of wooden components had not been built as the program called for. This applied to the construction areas in Thuringia, Silesia, and the Warthe District. Final assembly of the Ta 154s built in these areas was supposed to take place at assembly centers in Posen-Kreising, Erfurt, and Bunzlau. In the beginning the final assembly of large numbers of Ta 154s was also planned in Sorau or Cottbus, however, this too did not proceed as planned.

A great deal of room had been made for the Ta 154 in Delivery Program 223/1 of 15 April 1943. Large-scale production was supposed to begin in October 1943 and was to be increased in stages to 600 machines in January 1945. This increase in production of the Ta 154 was supposed to be accompanied by the cessation of production of the Ju 88 G-1, Bf 110 G-4, and Do 217 N-1/N-2 and their sub-variants. From June 1945 the Ta 154 and He 219 were to be the only night fighters in production. Production was expected to reach 200 aircraft per month by the end of 1943, 300 per month from July 1944 and 500 Ta 154s by November 1944. So much for the plans, for on 6 May 1943 the *General der Jagdflieger* canceled all further development work associated with the Ta 154, especially that involving the B-model, as long as industry was unable to provide a raised canopy to improve poor visibility from the cockpit. Thus, the first 1,500 A- and B-model aircraft were to be used as heavy fighters or high-speed bombers only. Further, on 8 May 1943 the *Luftwaffe*'s Quartermaster-General laid down that following the conversion of the Ta 154 airframe to include a metal fuselage and modified cockpit, 150 Ta 154 B night fighters, 150 Ta 154 B heavy fighters, and 200 Ta 154 B high-speed bombers were to be delivered monthly. While the number of machines to be produced was now less than that of the recent program plans, these production figures, too, were highly illusory.

Industry Program No. 223 of 18 June 1943 anticipated a total of 6,598

Ta 154 equipped with the Lichtenstein radar array.

Front view of WerkNr. 120005 (TQ+XE).

This Ta 154 A-0 (TQ+XE) was later rebuilt as an A-4.

Ta 154s by August 1945. Initially the bulk of these were to be the new A-1 and A-2 series, which were to be replaced by the significantly improved Ta 154 C-1, C-2 and C-4 by the end of 1945.

The problem with the glue manufacture significantly hampered the project's progress. Professor Tank therefore had no other choice than to place the machine's future in question. As a result of this one fanatical company member denounced him to the local G*auleiter*, accusing him of sabotage, and initiated a trial against him.

The RLM, however, assumed that this had to be a case of higher power at work and placed no blame for the delays on Kurt Tank. Early in August 1943 Kurt Tank gave a detailed report on the state of Ta 154 development to L*uftwaffe* commander-in-chief Göring, *Generalfeldmarschall* Milch, and his staff. Tank brought the problems with the wooden construction into the open, but not to their full extent.

According to Kurt Tank, large-scale production was supposed to begin in March 1944, which meant that approximately 500 Ta 154s, including the preproduction aircraft, could be built by the end of the year. This figure was significantly lower than those contained in the previous plans, but at the same time it was on shaky ground because of the many technical problems facing the project. The E-*Stelle Rechlin* was able to make a full assessment of the Ta 154 V1 by 22 November 1943. Hptm. Lichtfelder came to the conclusion that the prototype made a good overall impression but that the front-line units would be incapable of repairing damage to fuselages, wings, or tail assemblies. Since the wooden construction depended on precision work, aircraft carpenters were to be employed by Focke-Wulf immediately so that after the introductory phase they would themselves be able to carry out subsequent repairs or conversions at the unit level.

Difficulties with the strived-for large-scale production escalated to such a degree, however, that on 15 January 1944 (during an inspection of production facilities in Posen) the Plenipotentiary-General for the Employment of Labor Forces, *Gauleiter* Fritz Sauckel, threatened to send the local director Schnebel to a concentration camp should he fail to put the Ta 154 into production according to plan. However, the professed figures were much too optimistic to be realistic. An aligning of the Aircraft Program 225 and the plans of the Fighter Staff on 16 March 1944 showed that the first "production" Ta 154 from Erfurt could not be expected until May 1944. The first Silesian-built Ta 154 would be delivered in May 1944. At the same time, in Thuringia they were already thinking about the production of ten aircraft. Another 25 Ta 154s were supposed to leave the Focke-Wulf repair works near Erfurt. These plans also proved unrealistic, however.

In May 1944 production of the Ta 154 was supposed to proceed as follows: 102 Ta 154 A-1s had to be produced in the Posen area, and 410 A-1/R-1s in all three production areas, in order to reach the planned output figures. 165 A-4 night fighters were to be built in Thuringia. Construction of the Ta 154 C-1 was planned in the Posen area and in Erfurt. Final assembly of the C-3 was to take place simultaneously in Bunzlau and Erfurt. Since the start-up of work by the manufacturing areas was not showing the desired—or, more importantly quick—success, an effort was made to bolster series production by incorporating Focke-Wulf (Posen), the Erfurt repair facility, and the Weser Flugzeugwerken. Aircraft Program 226 of 15 May 1944 assumed that fourteen A-0 machines would be delivered, eleven of which had been completed by 30 April. Final assembly of the remaining three was to take place in May and June 1944. Focke-Wulf would manufacture 102 examples of the two-seat Ta 154 A-1 in the Posen area. All three production circles were to begin final assembly of the Ta 154 A-1/R1 day fighter, which was equipped with Jumo 211 N engines and GM 1, in September 1944. A total of 410 machines were supposed to be completed by February 1945. In addition, 157 examples of the Ta 154

The design of the Ta 154's cockpit resulted in a less than ideal view from the pilot's position.

Close-up view of the defensive position with MG 81 Z.

The Ta 154 V7 at Hannover-Langenhagen in April 1944.

A-2, a heavy fighter with Jumo 211 engines, were to be built.

Simultaneously the Gen*eral der Kampfflieger* and the *Technische Amt*, Departments GL/C and E7, did everything possible to transform the desired concept into reality as quickly as possible. In mid-May 1944 the design bureau presented revised planning studies for a "*Pulkzerstörer*" (formation destroyer), the Ta 154 A-0/U2. Since the Ta 154 was a machine with few light metal components, the design met with some favor. Professor Kurt Tank proposed the conversion of fifteen Ta 154 As.

In spite of this modest figure, only five aircraft were to be modified into the company's proposed "P*ulkzerstörer*" in the Posen factory. The first machine selected to serve as prototype for the new version, a Ta 154 A-0 with the *Werknummer* 120004, flew for the first time on 5 August 1944. It was destroyed in the air raid on Langenhagen on 5 August 1944 before it could be converted into an A-0/U2 "*Sondereinsatz*". Four additional machines, originally planned as Ta 154 A-0/U1 night fighters, were also scheduled for conversion. They were the aircraft that were supposed to be delivered between July and October 1944 with the following *Werknummern*: 0020 (old), 12011 (new); 0022 (old), 12001 (new); 0033 (old), 120060 (new); and 0034 (old), 120104 (new). According to the Ta 154 Prototype and Production Aircraft Overview of 31 May 1944, this "*Pulkzerstörer*" was to be powered by two Jumo 211 N power plants driving VS 11 propellers. A "*Sondereinbau*" (explosive charge) was to be installed in the forward fuselage. Electronics equipment consisted of a FuG 16 ZY and a simplified autopilot.

It may be assumed with certainty that the explosives carrier was not installed. There is no reference to this special version in the files of either the Fighter Staff or the Chief of Air Armaments, since Allied air superiority made it highly unlikely that such special missions would succeed.

In 1944 there was also a lack of unanimity concerning the possible use of the planned "Mi*stel Ta 154 A – Fw 190 A-8*," the "*Beethoven*" device. On 4 April 1944 the *Generalfeldmarschall* Milch, the *Generalluftzeugmeister* (head of *Luftwaffe* procurement), made a general statement against the use of valuable aircraft for *Mistel* operations. He subsequently instructed the *General der Kampfflieger* (GdK) and his GL/C-E2 and GL/C-E7 departments to compile a catalogue of requirements for *Mistel* operations. In contrast to the "*Pulkzerstörer*", the purpose of the "*Mistel*" was to strike important ground targets.

After completion of the necessary sets of drawings in May 1944 and the equipment lists in June, on 14 July 1944 a brief specification was drawn up for a Ta 154 as unmanned explo-

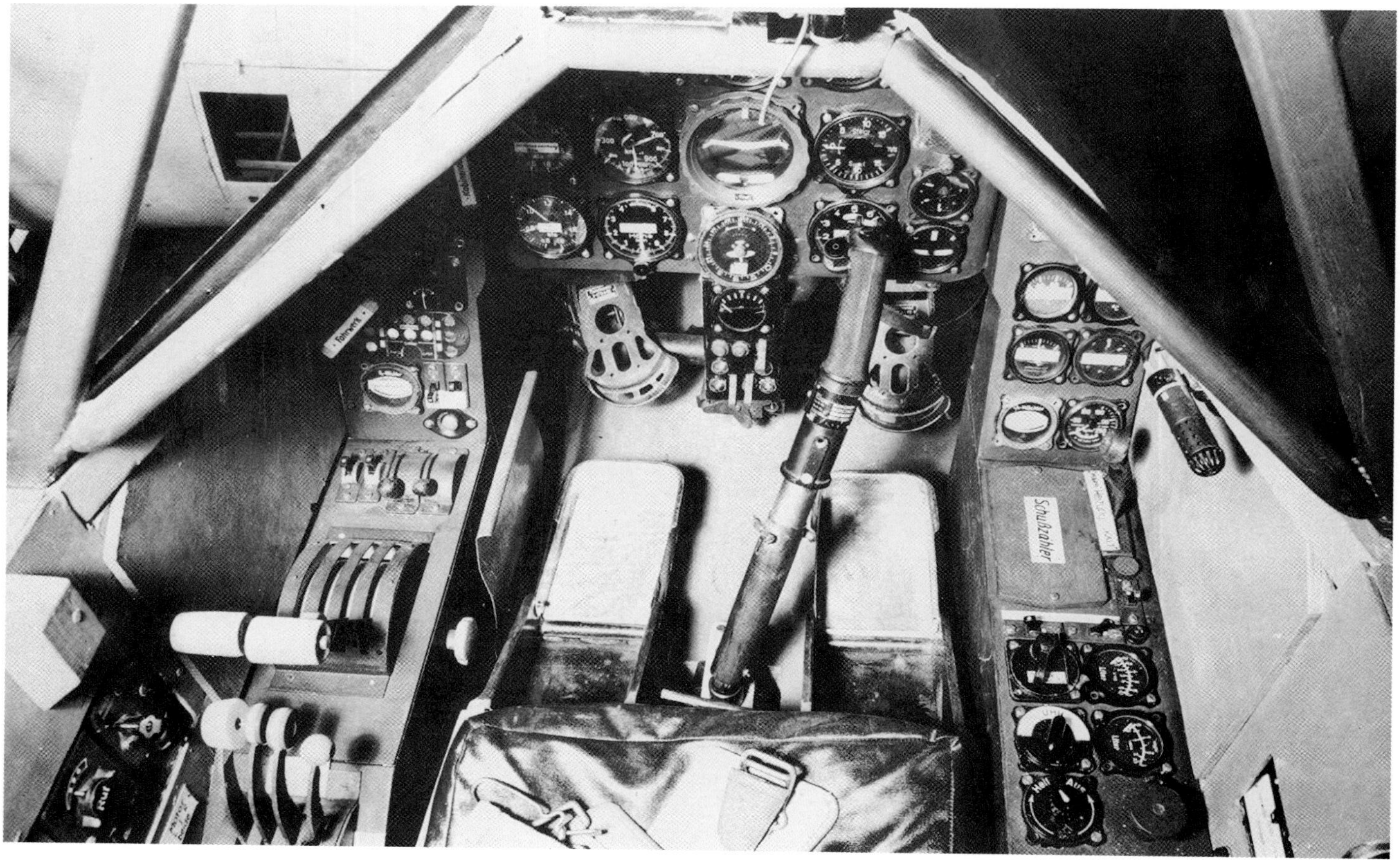

The Ta 154 cockpit mock-up was modified several times.

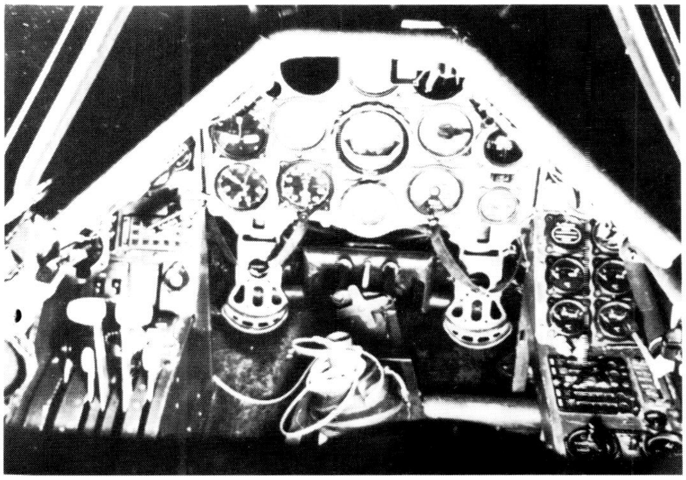

The Ta 154 A-0's instrument panel.

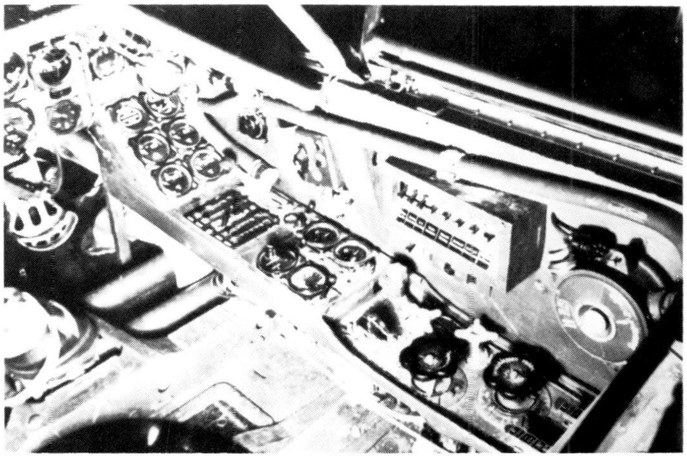

The portside console with oxygen equipment.

sives carrier with a cradle-mounted Fw 190 A-8 as control aircraft. Now, instead of "*Pulkzerstörer*", four "*Beethoven-Gespanne*" (Beethoven combinations) were to be built in the Posen factory. Focke-Wulf assumed that the device, whose maximum weight was 15,150 kg, would be able to take off from a concrete runway. Operation and control of the *Mistel* would have been identical to the Ju 88 *Mistel* in all respects.

Calculations were made for three versions, which differed only in the size of their hollow-charge warheads (2,500 kg, 3,000 kg and 3,500 kg). Based on previous estimates of structural strength and in view of the Ta 154's undercarriage only the use of the 2,500-kg charge was considered. Preparations for construction were supposed to start in Posen at the end of July 1944. Prior to this, on 17 July there was a discussion between the RLM and Professor Tank concerning this unusual aircraft. It was determined that a 2,500-kg warhead, whose design would be guided by the RLM, was to be installed in the aircraft. In order to reduce installation time at future bases of operation to a minimum, the combinations were to be delivered there without warheads. Ferry flights with the warhead installed would have required some strengthening of the undercarriage, since the combination's landing weight would have been in the range of 12,500 kg. The RLM saw the use of a takeoff trolley as the ultimate solution. Focke-Wulf was directed to begin construction at once, taking advantage of Junkers' experience. According to *Ingenieur* Scheibe a written contract would soon follow. The company assumed that the first combinations would be ready for delivery by the end of August 1944. It expected to build a total of fifty Mistel aircraft. Work proceeded with a high degree of urgency until mid-August. But then an order was received to convert the first four aircraft into night fighters

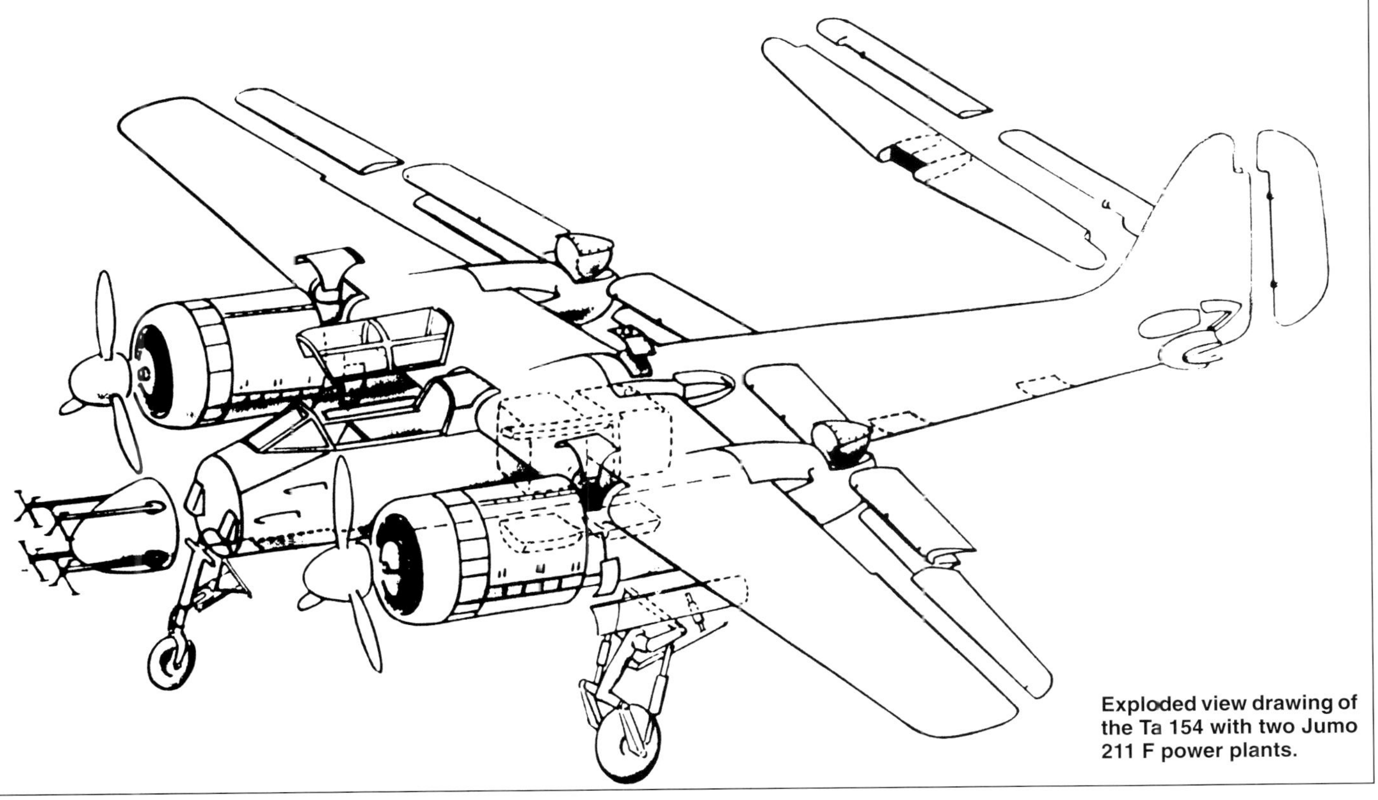

Exploded view drawing of the Ta 154 with two Jumo 211 F power plants.

Nosewheel retraction mechanism.

with Jumo 213 engines and employ them experimentally. According to Hans Sander, neither the "*Pulkzerstörer*" nor "*Mistelgespann*" ever flew.

Conclusions

Total production of the Ta 154 amounted to just twelve flyable aircraft plus five static test airframes. Furthermore, a maximum of seven pre-production (Ta 154 A-0) and about twelve production aircraft were built. Some of these machines were converted several times and thus reappeared with new type designations.

Of the production aircraft, *Werknummern* 320008 to 320011 are known for the Ta 154 A-2/U4 night and bad weather fighter version. A-4 night fighters equipped with FuG 220 airborne radar and bearing the *Werknummern* 320005, 320006, 320013 and 320015 are said to have been built. The war prevented the final assembly of some of these machines and consequently they were scrapped before they ever flew.

On 7 November 1944 the *General der Jagdflieger* canceled the six Ta 154s which *Hauptdienstleiter* Sauer was supposed to provide for test purposes. It cannot be determined with certainty that these were night fighters. Of those Ta 154s that were delivered, eight fell victim to crashes and crash landings. Another nine machines were destroyed or seriously damaged at Langenhagen as a result of enemy action. A tenth Ta 154 (WerkNr. 120015) survived the attack with minor damage. In addition to these machines, the design mock-up was damaged by debris. Only a single Ta 154 A-2 remained at Langenhagen until the end of the war.

After the fuel ran out, several of the aircraft delivered to NJG 3 were sim-

One Ta 154 A-1 served with III.(Erg.)/JG 2 in Lechfeld as a training aircraft.

Side view of the two-seat trainer.

The Ta 154 as found at Lechfeld behind a stack of jet engines waiting to be scrapped.

Ta 154 airframe under construction.

Main undercarriage of a Ta 154.

Engine cowling with bulged fairing for the flame damper.

Ta 154 A-2/U4
of Stab III/NJG 3.

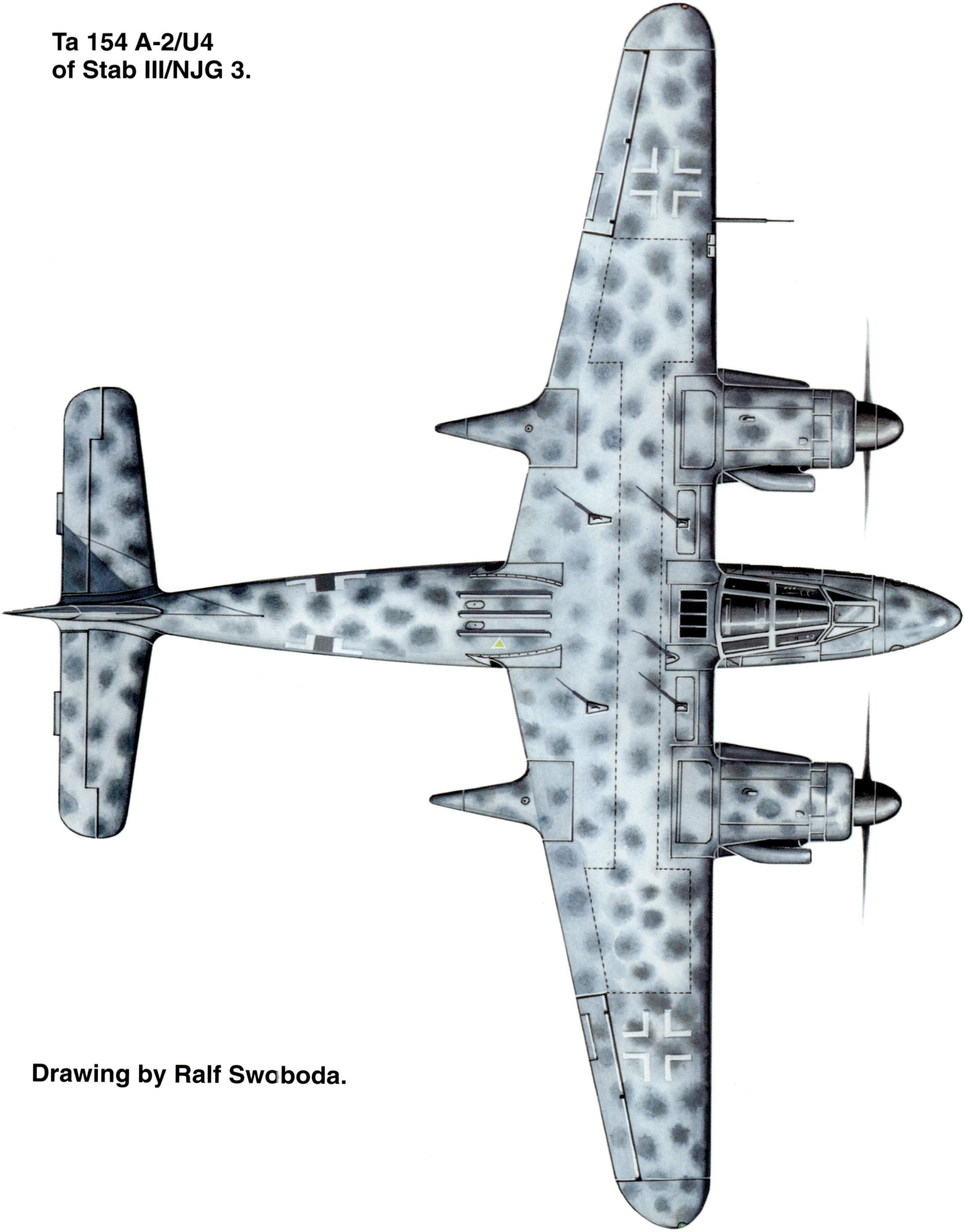

Drawing by Ralf Swoboda.

D5
HD

D5
HD

Press used to shape metal engine cowling panels.

The few operational examples of the Ta 154 had the radar antennas mounted in the wing center-section.

ply pushed to the edge of the airfield and left there. At least three of these Ta 154 were blown up by III/NJG 3 at the end of April 1945. The machine parked at Lechfeld, and the numerous components and parts captured by the Allies were the only evidence of the great efforts made to match the British D.H. Mosquito.

In the end, the unsolvable problem of finding a satisfactory glue with which to build the Ta 154, but also the unavailability of Jumo 213 engines and various design weaknesses in the area of the undercarriage and hydraulics, resulted in just thirty Ta 154s being built.

Translated from the German by Ed Force

Printed in China.
ISBN: 0-7643-0911-0

This book was originally published under the title,
Flugzeug Profile: Tank Ta 154 - Die Geschichte des deutschen Mosquito
by Flugzeug Publikations, GmBH.

We are interested in hearing from authors with book ideas on related topics.

Schiffer Military History
Atglen, PA

Published by Schiffer Publishing Ltd.
4880 Lower Valley Road
Atglen, PA 19310
Phone: (610) 593-1777
FAX: (610) 593-2002
E-mail: Schifferbk@aol.com
Please visit our online catalog at www.schifferbooks.com
Please write for a free catalog.
This book may be purchased from the publisher.
Please include $3.95 postage.
Try your bookstore first.

Ta 154

Type	Old WerkNr.	New WerkNr	Registration	First flight/First mention
Ta 154 V1	1540000001	100001	TE+FE	01/07/1943
Ta 154 V2	0002	100002	TE+FF	10/09/1943
Ta 154 V3	0003	100003	TE+FG	25/11/1943
Ta 154 V4	0004	100004	TE+FH	19/01/1944
Ta 154 V5	0005	100005	TE+FI	25/02/1944
Ta 154 V6	0006	100006	TE+FJ	18/03/1944
Ta 154 V7	0007	100007	TE+FK	25/03/1944
Ta 154 V8	0008	100008	TE+FL	08/04/1944
Ta 154 V9	0009	100009	TE+FM	18/04/1944
Ta 154 V10	0010	100010	TE+FN	04/06/1944
Ta 154 V22	0011	120001	TQ+XA	12/06/1944
Ta 154 A-0	0012	120002	TQ+XB	16/04/1944
Ta 154 V23	0013	120003	TQ+XC	14/07/1944
Ta 154 A-0	0014	120004	TQ+XD	25/05/1944
Ta 154 A-0	0015	120005	TQ+XE	30/06/1944
Ta 154 A-0	0016	120006	TQ+XF	not known
Ta 154 A-0	0017	120007	—	—
Ta 154 A-0	0018	120008	—	—
Ta 154 A-0	0019	120009	TQ+XI	not known
Ta 154 A-0	0020	120010	—	—
Ta 154 A-0/U1	0021	120011	—	—
Ta 154 A-0/U1	0022	120012	—	—
Ta 154 A-0/U1	0023	120013	—	—
Ta 154 A-0/U1	0024	120014	TQ+XN	July 1944
Ta 154 A-0/U1	0025	120015	TQ+XO	July 1944
Ta 154 A-0/U1	0026	120056	—	—
Ta 154 A-0/U1	0027	120057	—	—
Ta 154 A-0/U1	0028	120058	—	—
Ta 154 A-0/U1	0029	120059	not known	not known
Ta 154 A-0/U1	0030	120060	—	—
Ta 154 A-0/U1	0031	120101	—	—
Ta 154 A-0/U1	0032	120102	—	—
Ta 154 A-0/U1	0033	120103	—	—
Ta 154 A-0/U1	0034	120104	—	—
Ta 154 C-1	0035	120105	—	—
Ta 154 C-2	0036	120106	—	—
Ta 154 A-1		320002	KU+SO	12/06/1944
Ta 154 A-1		320004	KU+SP	June 1944
Ta 154 A-1		320005	—	—
Ta 154 A-1		320006	KU+SS	06/07/1944
Ta 154 A-1		320007	KU+ST	July 1944
Ta 154 A-2		320008	KU+SU	01/08/1944
Ta 154 A-2		320009	KU+SV	01/08/1944
Ta 154 A-2		320010	KU+SW	14/08/1944
Ta 154 A-2		320011	KU+SX	28/08/1944
Ta 154 A-2		320012	—	—
Ta 154 A-2		320013	—	—
Ta 154 A-2		320014	—	—
Ta 154 A-2		320015	—	—
Ta 154 A-2		320016	—	—
Ta 154 A-2		320017	—	Aug 1944
Ta 154 A-2		320018	—	—
Ta 154 A-2		320059	not known	not known

Ta 154 – List of Variants

Ta 154 A-0	night fighter (two-seat)	Jumo 211 N with VS 11
Ta 154 A-0/U1	night fighter (two-seat)	Jumo 211 N with VS 11
Ta 154 A-0/U2	Pulkzerstörer (single-seat)	Jumo 211 N with VS 11
Ta 154 A-1	day fighter (single-seat)	Jumo 211 N/R
Ta 154 A-1/R1	day fighter (two-seat)	Jumo 211 N and GM 1
Ta 154 A-2	day fighter (single-seat)	Jumo 211 N/R and GM 1
Ta 154 A-2/U4	night and bad weather fighter (two seat)	Jumo 211 N/R
Ta 154 A-3	training aircraft (two-seat)	Jumo 211 N/R
Ta 154 A-4	night fighter (two-seat)	Jumo 211 N/R
Ta 154 B-1	night fighter (two-seater)	Jumo 211 N with VS 9
Ta 154 B-2	day fighter (single-seat)	Jumo 211 N with VS 9
Ta 154 C-1	night fighter (two-seat)	Jumo 213 A with VS 111
Ta 154 C-2	day fighter and fighter-bomber	Jumo 213 A with VS 111 (single-seat)
Ta 154 C-3	day fighter (two-seat)	Jumo 213 A with VS 111
Ta 154 D-1[1]	high-altitude fighter	Jumo 213 E with VS 111 (two-seat)

Ta 254 Variants

Ta 254 A-0	night fighter (two-seat)	Jumo 213 E with VS 9
Ta 254 A-1	night fighter (two-seat)	Jumo 213 E with VS 9
Ta 254 A-2	day fighter (single-seat)	Jumo 213 E with VS 9
Ta 254 A-3	day fighter (single-seat)	Jumo 213 E without MW 50
Ta 254 B-1	night fighter	DB 603 L
Ta 254 B-2	day fighter	Jumo 212 F or G
Ta 254 B-3	day fighter	DB 603 L, MW 50 Rüstsatz

[1] signated as the Ta 254

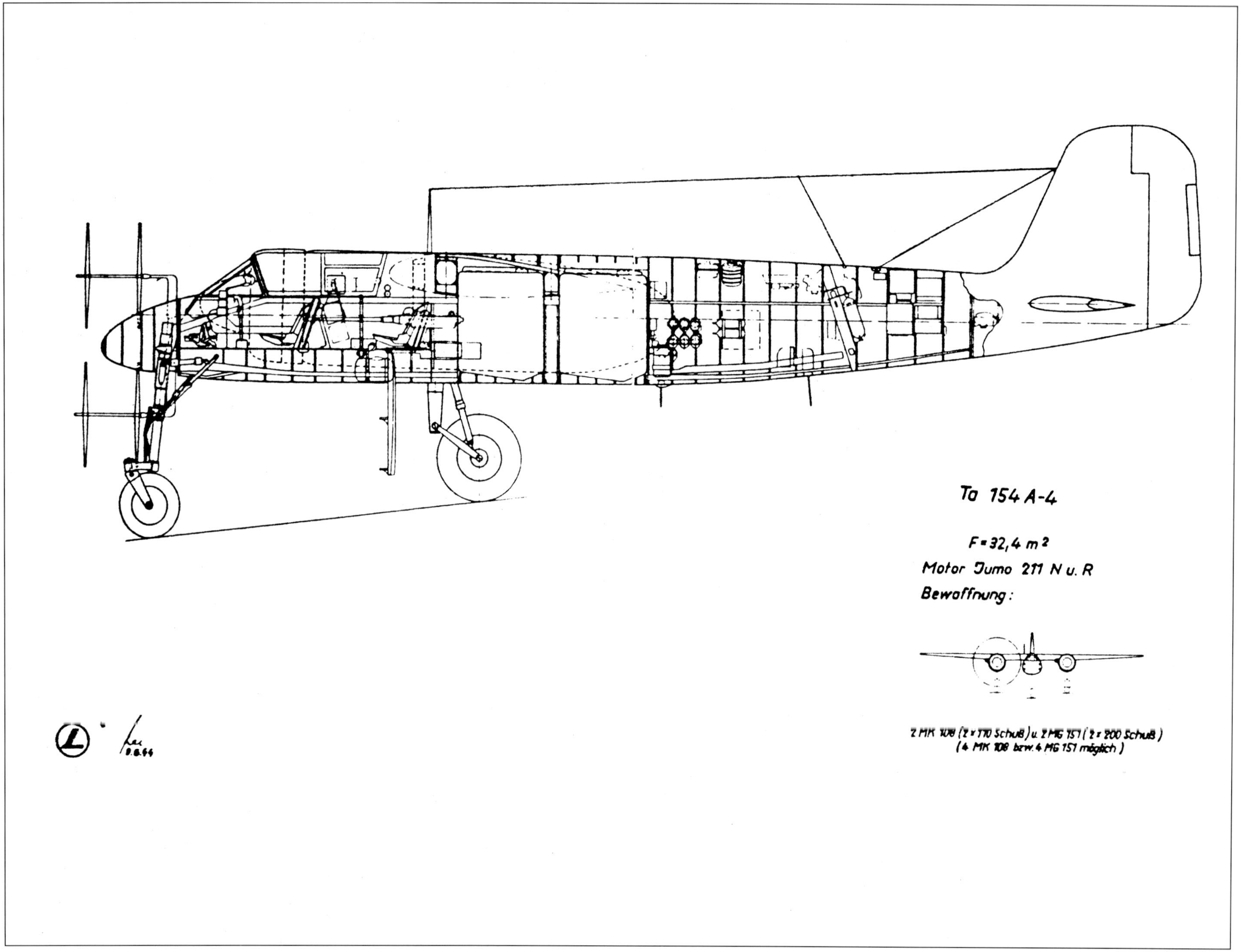
Ta 154 A-4
F = 32,4 m²
Motor Jumo 211 N u. R
Bewaffnung:
2 MK 108 (2 x 110 Schuß) u. 2 MG 151 (2 x 200 Schuß)
(4 MK 108 bzw. 4 MG 151 möglich)
9.8.44

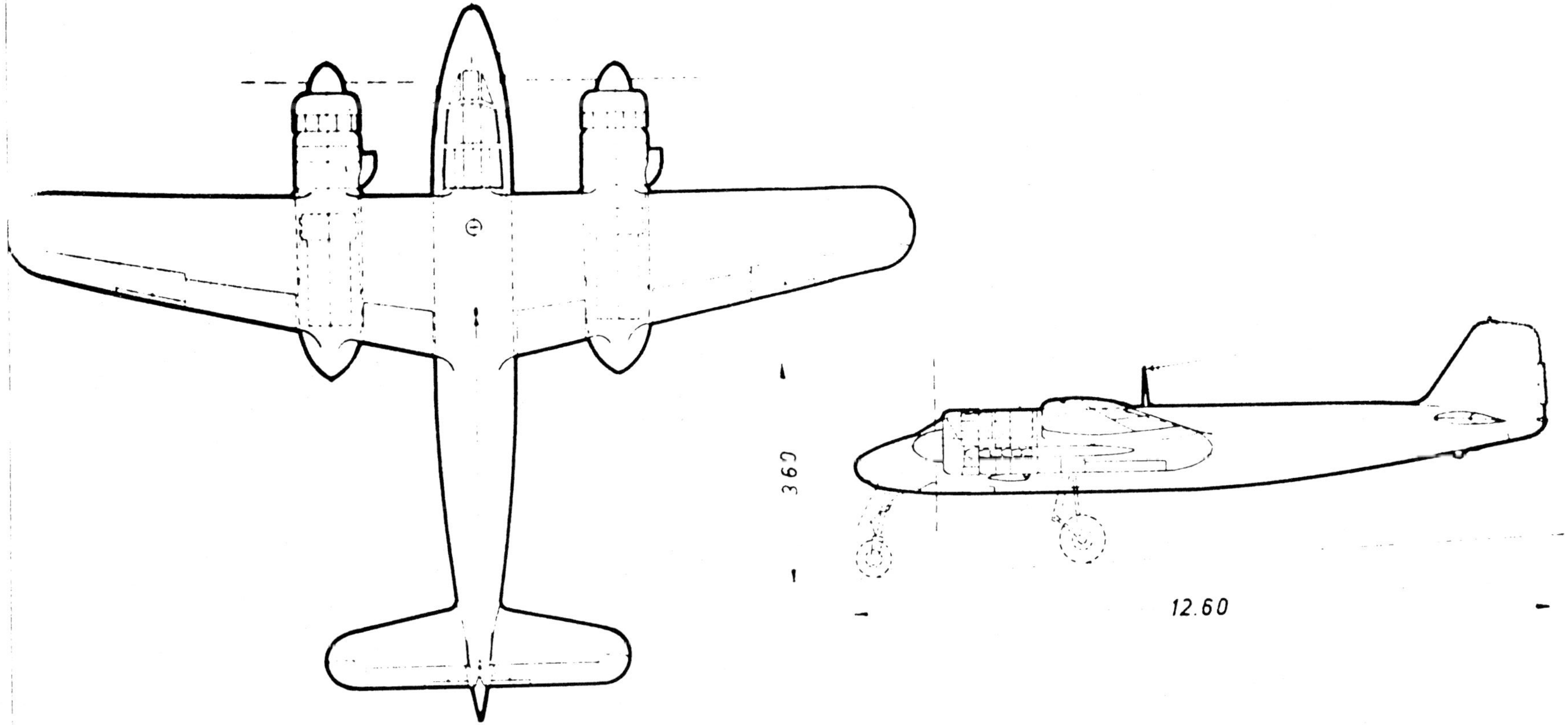

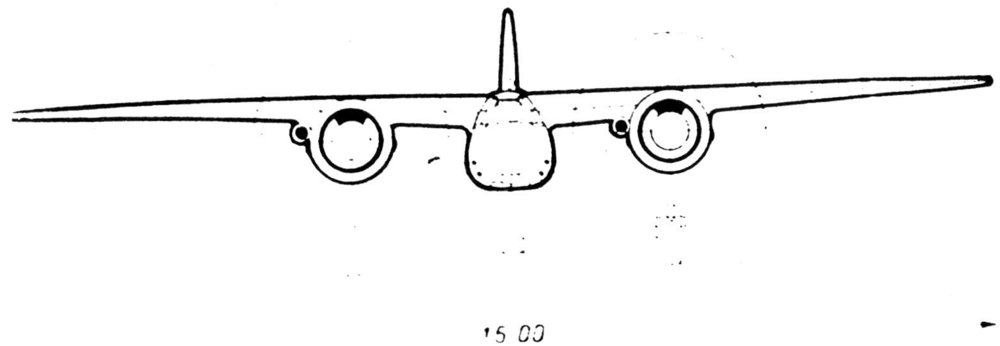

Ta 154 A

Version	Zweck	Bes.	Motor	Bew.
A-1	Tagjagd	2	Jumo 211N	2 MG 151 2 MK 108
A-2	"	1	" " R	"
A-3	"	2	" " R	"
A-4	Nachtjagd	2	" " R	+2 MK 108

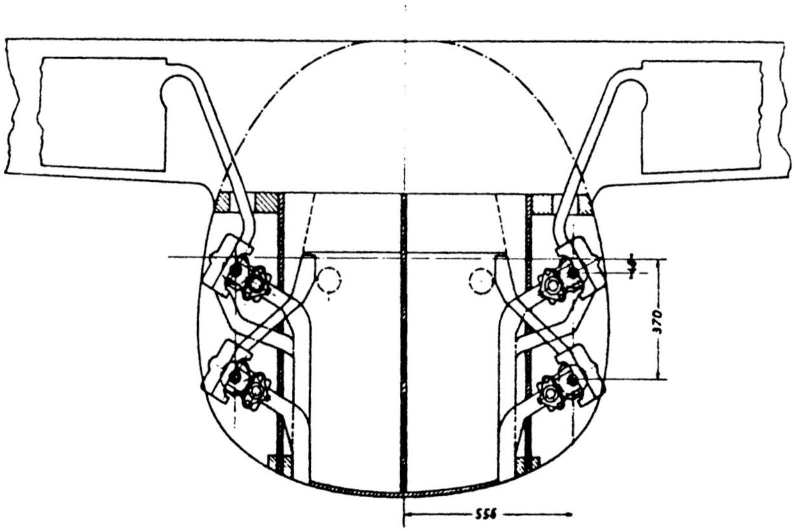

4 MG 151 mit je 200 Schuß

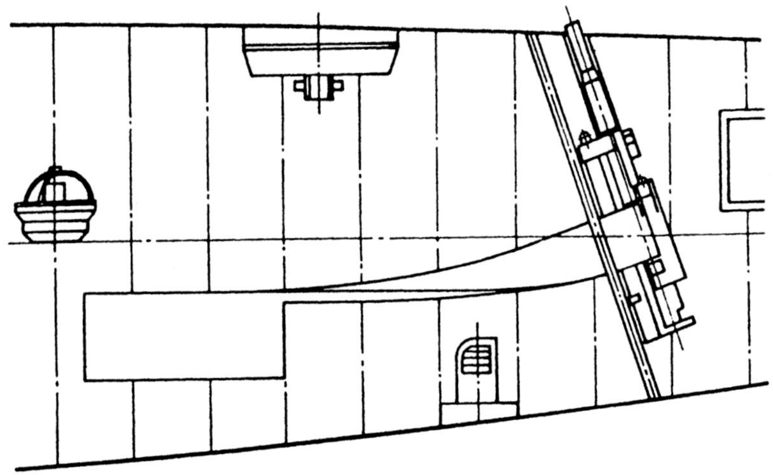

1 MK mit 100-145 Schuß

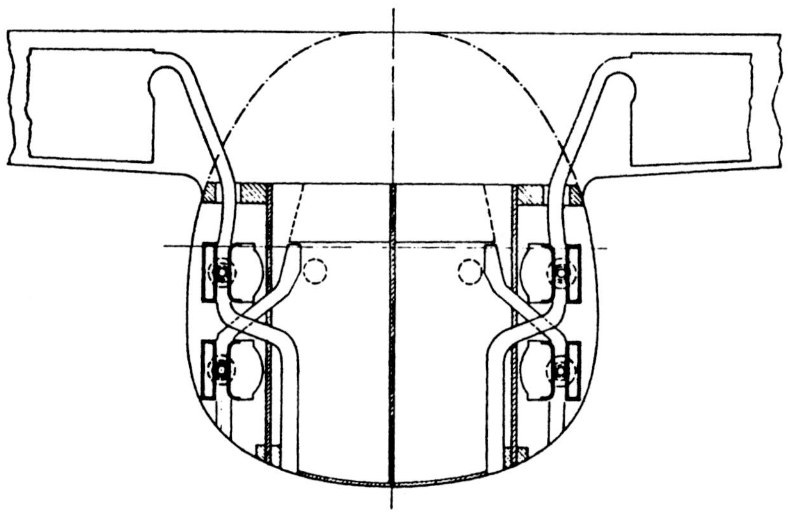

oder 4 MK 108 mit je 100-110 Schuß

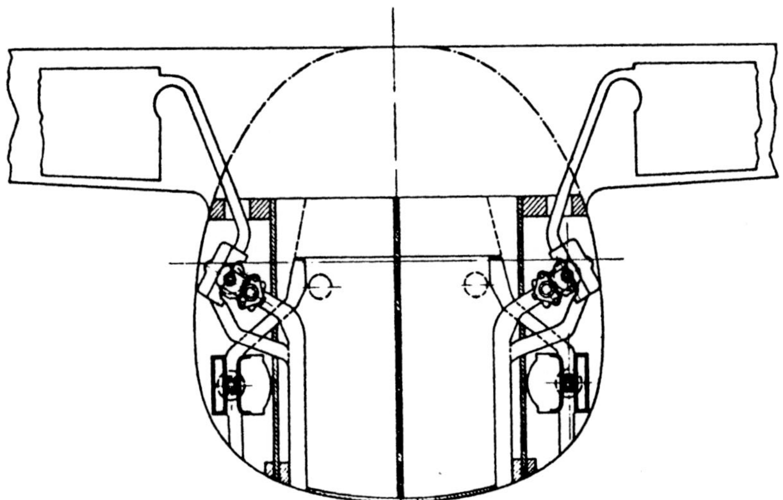

oder 2 MG 151 mit je 200 Schuß
2 MK 108 mit je 100-110 Schuß

Nachtjäger Ta 154
mit 2 x Jumo 211 F
Bewaffnung

Junkers Flugzeug- und -Motorenwerke Aktiengesellschaft JFM-Motorenvertrieb	*Zerstörer-Triebwerk J 213 A-1/C-1* *Gerät Nr. 9-8213 C-1*

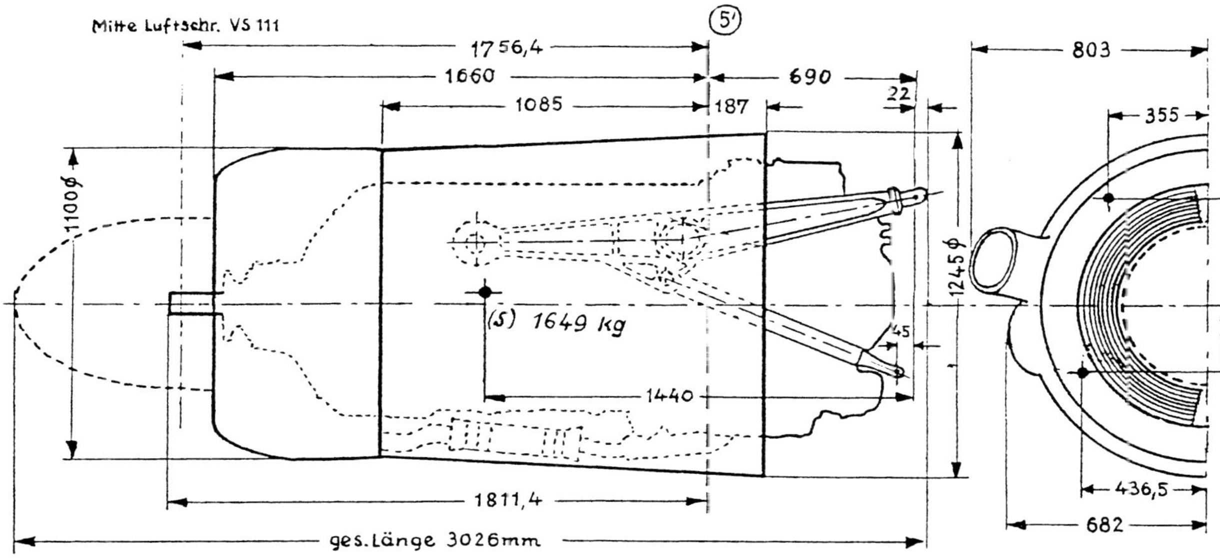

Motor:	JUMO 213 A-1
Luftschraube:	Junkers VS 111 3,50 m ⌀ b/d = 10,5 %
Flugzeug:	Ta 154 C (2 motorig)

Triebwerks-Lieferumfang:

Flugmotor mit Anbau- und Verbindungsteilen	9-8213.200-000
Motorträger	9-8213.210-000
Kühleranbau m. Panzerung Serienausführung	9-8213.299-000
Kühleranbau ohne Panzerung	8213.298-000
Kühlstoffanlage	9-8213.240-000
Abgasmischanlage	9-8213.245-000
Elt-Anlage	9-8213.250-000
Triebwerks-Ausrüstung	9-8213.256-000
Hydr. Anlage	9-8213.260-000
Verbindungs-Untergruppen	9-8213.266-000
Motorverkleidung	9-8213.271-000

Triebwerks-Gewichte:

Triebwerks-Trockengewicht (Lieferumfang)		1306,5 kg
Kühlstoff	73,5 kg	
Schmierstoff	18,- kg	
Kraftstoff	2,- kg	
Hydrauliköl	2,- kg	95,5 kg
Luftschraubennabe	141,- kg	
3 Blätter	94,5 kg	
Luftschraubenhaube	11,5 kg	247,- kg
Triebwerks-Einbaugewicht		1649,- kg + 3 %

Rüstsätze

Berechnungsgrundlagen:

Wasserkühler: Stirnkühler. Wirksame Stirnfläche 49 dm^2, 135 mm tief
Bauart: SKF - Leichtmetall - Scheidenkühler geschlitzt ausgelegt für 365 000 kcal/h bei Steig- und Kampfleistung in Volldruckhöhe. Bahngeschwindigkeit im Steigen (Bodennähe) v_a= 80 m/sec. Max. Außentemperatur +30°C + 5° Verschmutzung. Motor-Austrittstemperatur 100°C in allen Flughöhen, max. 120°C beim Rollen und Start.

Traggerüst: vertikales, sichere Abfanglastvielfaches $n_z = +7$
seitliches, sichere Lastvielfache $n_y = \pm 1{,}5$

Ex/Hoff.	1.4.1944		Blatt 8

Fw/Beg/17-9-43 ✓.

Focke-Wulf Flugzeugbau G.m.b.H. Bremen

Gewichtszusammenstellung

Blatt:

	Fluggewicht	Rüstgewicht	Leergewicht 1+)	Leergewicht 2+)
Fw 58 C1	2930	2220	1515	2075
Fw 58 C2	2930	2240	1535	2095
Fw 189 A0	3700	2970	1580	2430
Fw 189 A1	4000	3300	1840	2680
Fw 189 A2	4130	3350	1860	2700
Fw 200 C4	22700	14570	8070	11580
Fw 190 A1	3775	3100	1180	2590
Fw 190 A2	3850	3175	1225	2635
Fw 190 A5	3950	3235	1275	2685
Fw 190 F3 Schl. Fl.	4160	3445	1480	2890
Fw 190 G Jaborei	4890	3300	1310	2720
Ta 152 DB 60 3G	4400	3670	1450	2865
Ta 154 A0	8460	6900	3525	5790
Ta 154 A1	8260	6660	3325	5585
Ta 154 A2				
Ta 154 B1	9000	7360	3900	6160
Ta 154 B2				
Ta 154 C1	9920	8170	3970	6342
Ta 154 C2				
Ta 154 C3				
Ta 154 C4				

Focke-Wulf Flugzeugbau G.m.b.H. Nr. 26a

Bemerkungen:

1+) Das angegebene Leergewicht ist ermittelt aus dem Rüstgewicht abzüglich: Flugmotoren, Luftschrauben, Laufrädern, Federstreben. Geschützte Kraft- und Schmierstoffbehälter, Kühler, Betriebsleitungsfüllungen Ausrüstungsgeräte, Waffen.

2+) Das angegebene Leergewicht ist ermittelt aus dem Rüstgewicht abzüglich: geschützte Kraft- und Schmierstoffbehälter, Kühler, Betriebsleitungsfüllungen, Ausrüstungsgeräte, Waffen. Jedoch mit Motoren, Luftschrauben, Laufrädern, Federstreben.

Nach Aufstellung Begandt 10.9.43

Fw 4346

Bad Eilsen, d. 17.9.43	Mappe Nr.	Ausgegeben	

Fw 589

Nachtjäger Ta154
Führer-Gerätebretter

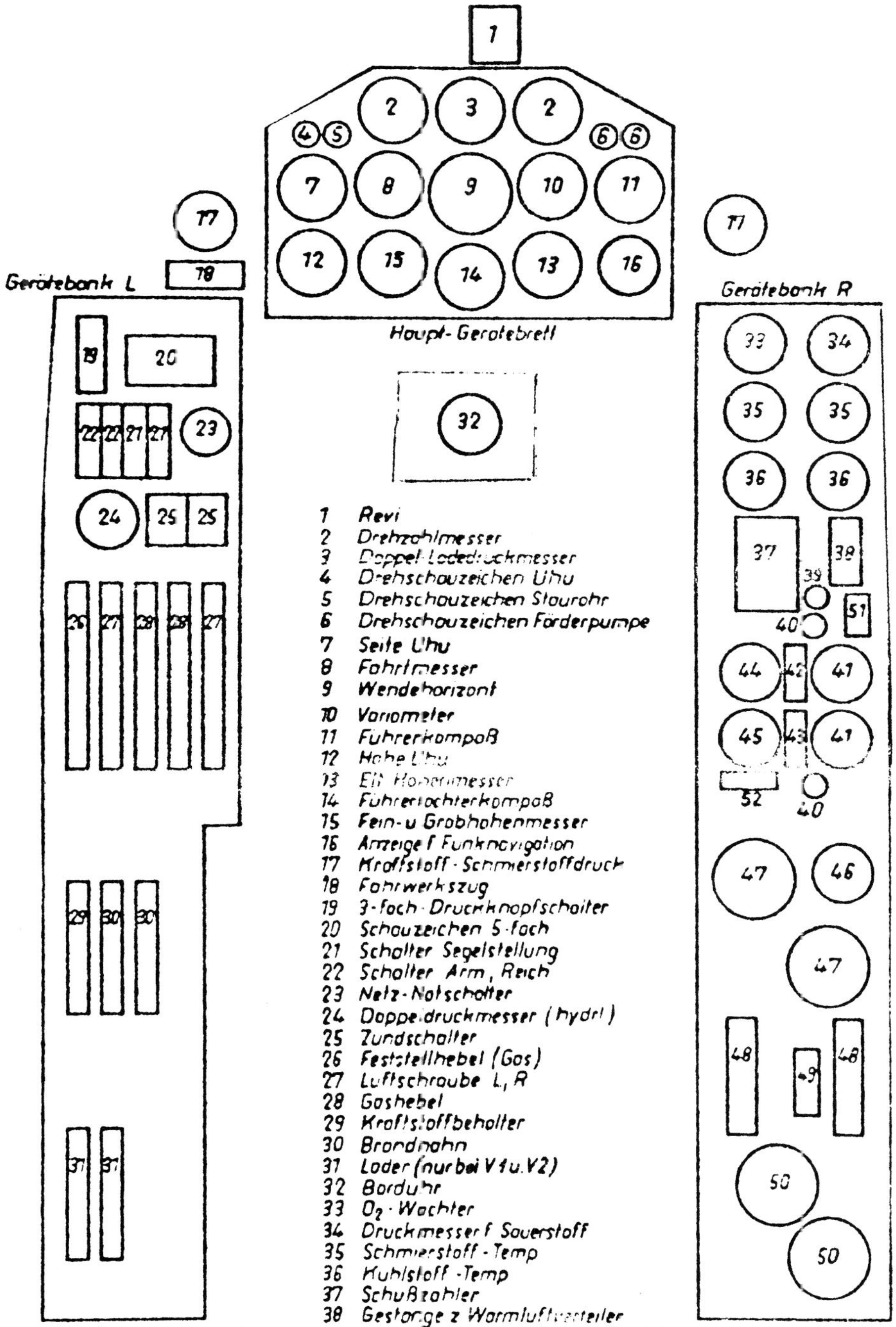

1 Revi
2 Drehzahlmesser
3 Doppel-Ladedruckmesser
4 Drehschauzeichen Uhu
5 Drehschauzeichen Staurohr
6 Drehschauzeichen Förderpumpe
7 Seite Uhu
8 Fahrtmesser
9 Wendehorizont
10 Variometer
11 Führerkompaß
12 Höhe Uhu
13 El. Höhenmesser
14 Führertochterkompaß
15 Fein-u Grobhöhenmesser
16 Anzeige f. Funknavigation
17 Kraftstoff - Schmierstoffdruck
18 Fahrwerkszug
19 3-fach-Druckknopfschalter
20 Schauzeichen 5-fach
21 Schalter Segelstellung
22 Schalter Arm, Reich
23 Netz-Notschalter
24 Doppeldruckmesser (hydr.)
25 Zündschalter
26 Feststellhebel (Gas)
27 Luftschraube L, R
28 Gashebel
29 Kraftstoffbehälter
30 Brandhahn
31 Lader (nur bei V1u.V2)
32 Borduhr
33 O_2-Wächter
34 Druckmesser f. Sauerstoff
35 Schmierstoff-Temp
36 Kühlstoff-Temp
37 Schußzähler
38 Gestänge z. Warmluftverteiler
39 Schauzeichen-Heizung
40 Merkleuchte für Kraftstoffvorrat
41 Kraftstoffvorrat
42 Kurssteuerung Hauptschalter
43 Kurssteuerung Notschalter
44 Kreiselüberwachungsschalter
45 Schalter Uhu
46 Durchgangsventil (Sauerstoff)
47 Drehschalter (hydr.)
48 Anlaßschalter
49 Einspritzschalter
50 Kühlerklappen-Verstellung
51 Schalter Kabinenheizung
52 Schalter Scheibenheizung

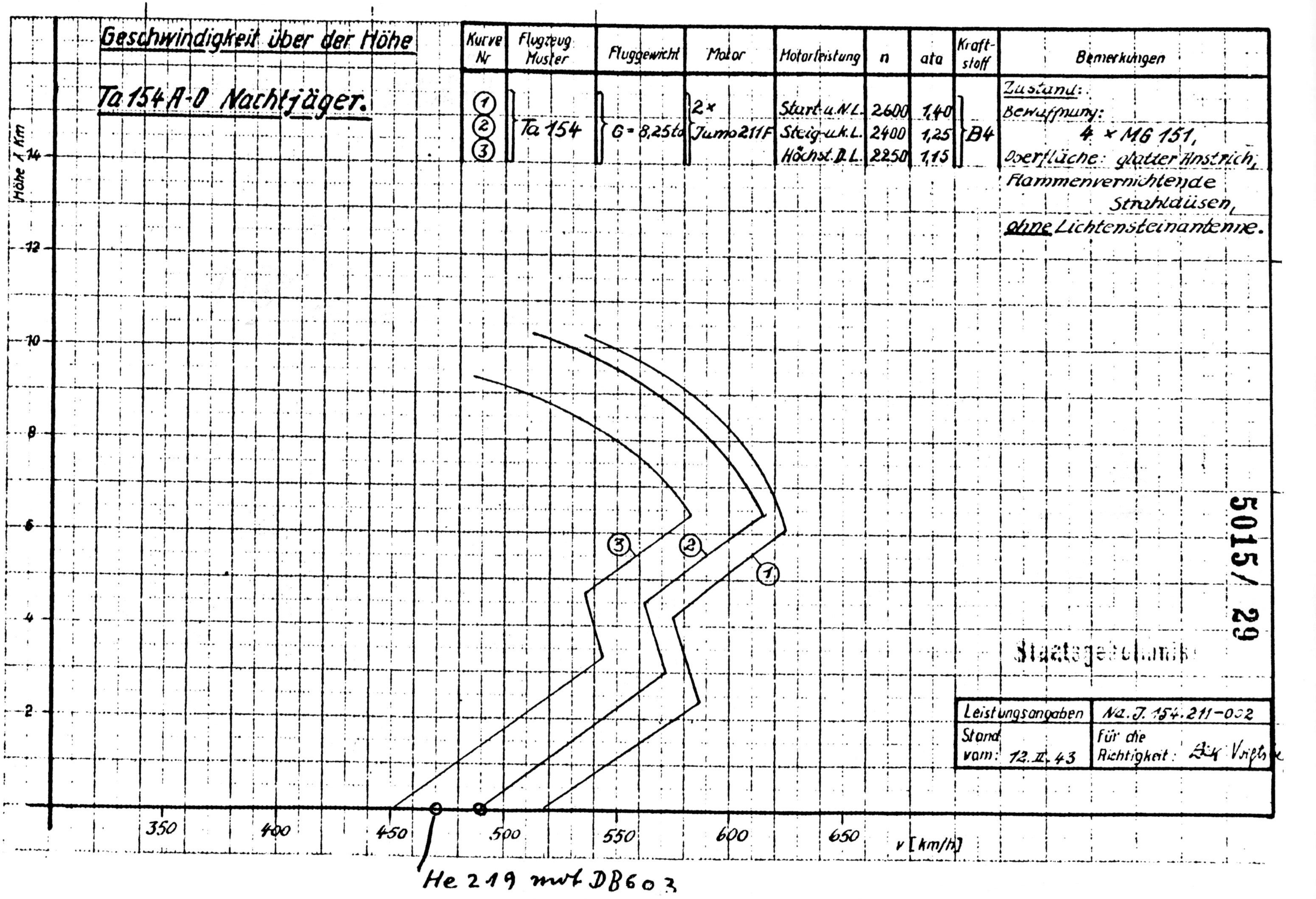

Geschwindigkeit über der Höhe
Ta 154 A-0 Nachtjäger.
Kurve Nr | Flugzeug Muster | Fluggewicht | Motor | Motorleistung | n | ata | Kraftstoff | Bemerkungen
1, 2, 3 | Ta 154 | G = 8,25 to | 2 × Jumo 211 F | Start u. N.L. 2600 1,40 | Steig- u. K.L. 2400 1,25 | Höchst. D.L. 2250 1,15 | B4
Zustand:
Bewaffnung:
4 × MG 151,
Oberfläche: glatter Anstrich,
Flammenvernichtende Strahldüsen,
ohne Lichtensteinantenne.
Höhe / Km
14
12
10
8
6
4
2
350
400
450
500
550
600
650
v [km/h]
5015/ 29
Leistungsangaben
Nr. J. 154. 211-002
Stand vom: 12. II. 43
Für die Richtigkeit:
He 219 mit DB 603

Focke-Wulf Ta 154 A

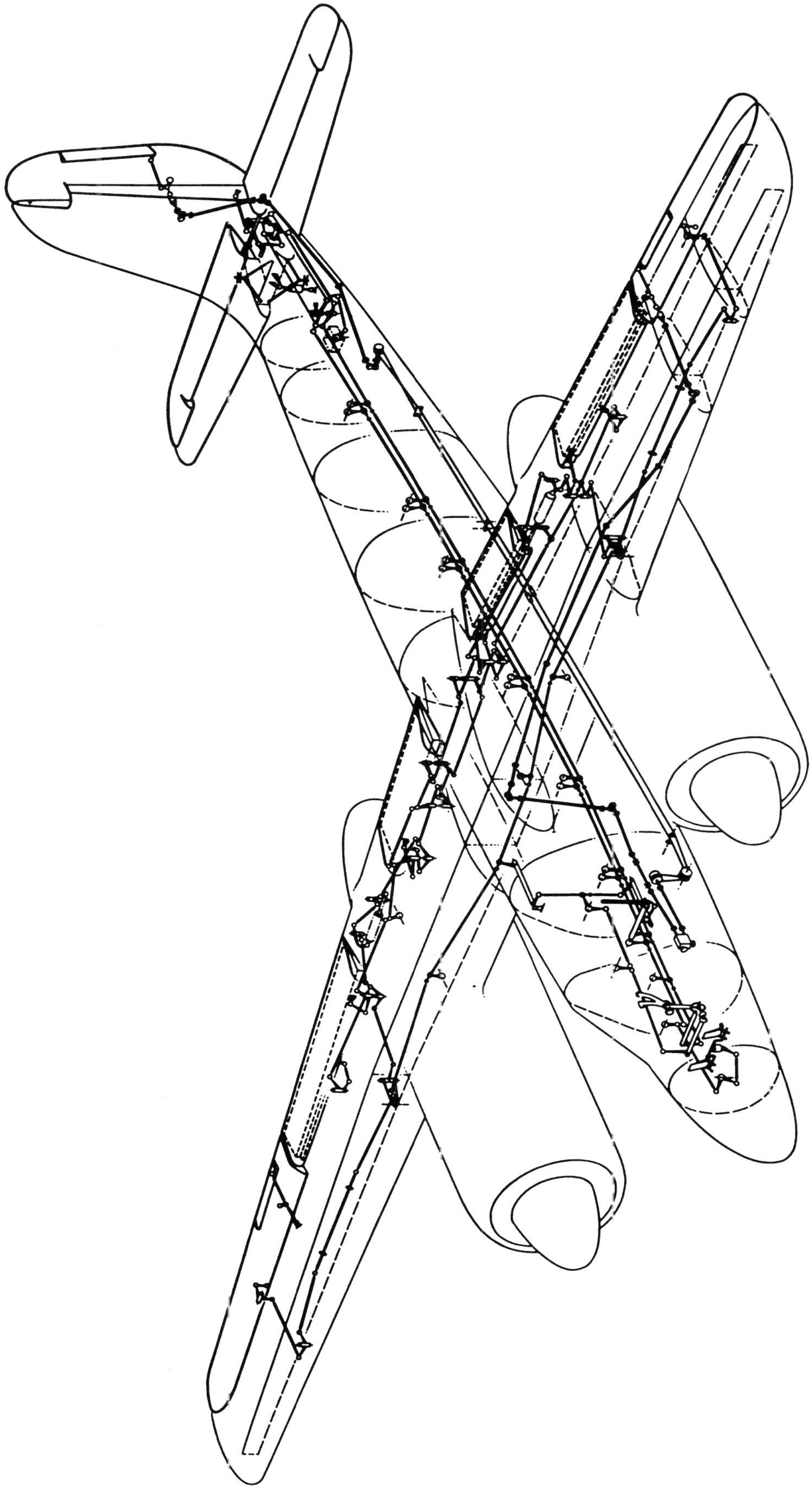

154.400

R 1452/458 v

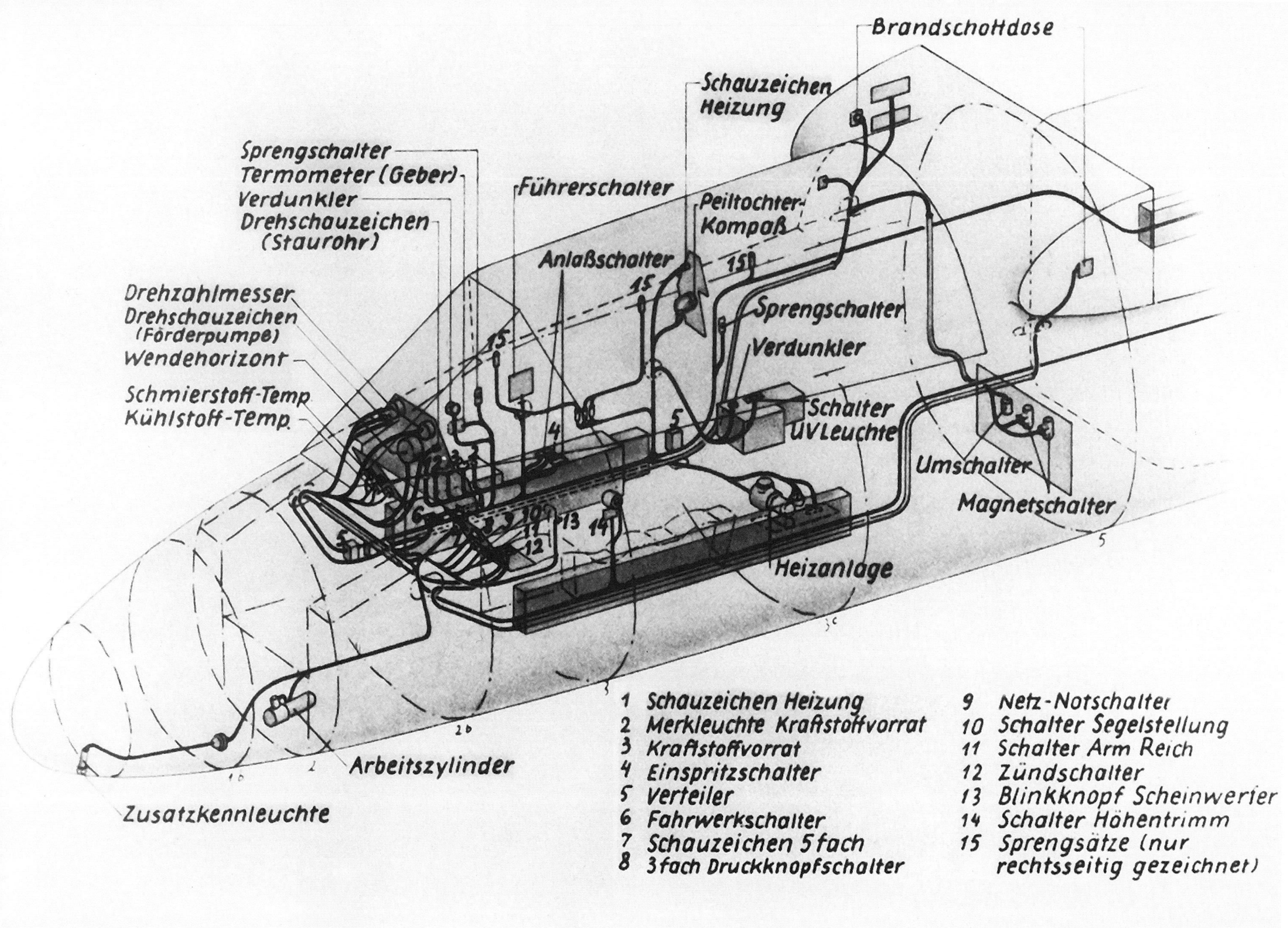
Brandschottdose
Schauzeichen Heizung
Sprengschalter
Termometer (Geber)
Verdunkler
Drehschauzeichen (Staurohr)
Führerschalter
Peiltochter-Kompaß
Anlaßschalter
Drehzahlmesser
Drehschauzeichen (Förderpumpe)
Wendehorizont
Schmierstoff-Temp
Kühlstoff-Temp.
Sprengschalter
Verdunkler
Schalter UV Leuchte
Umschalter
Magnetschalter
Heizanlage
Arbeitszylinder
Zusatzkennleuchte
1 Schauzeichen Heizung
2 Merkleuchte Kraftstoffvorrat
3 Kraftstoffvorrat
4 Einspritzschalter
5 Verteiler
6 Fahrwerkschalter
7 Schauzeichen 5fach
8 3fach Druckknopfschalter
9 Netz-Notschalter
10 Schalter Segelstellung
11 Schalter Arm Reich
12 Zündschalter
13 Blinkknopf Scheinwerfer
14 Schalter Höhentrimm
15 Sprengsätze (nur rechtsseitig gezeichnet)

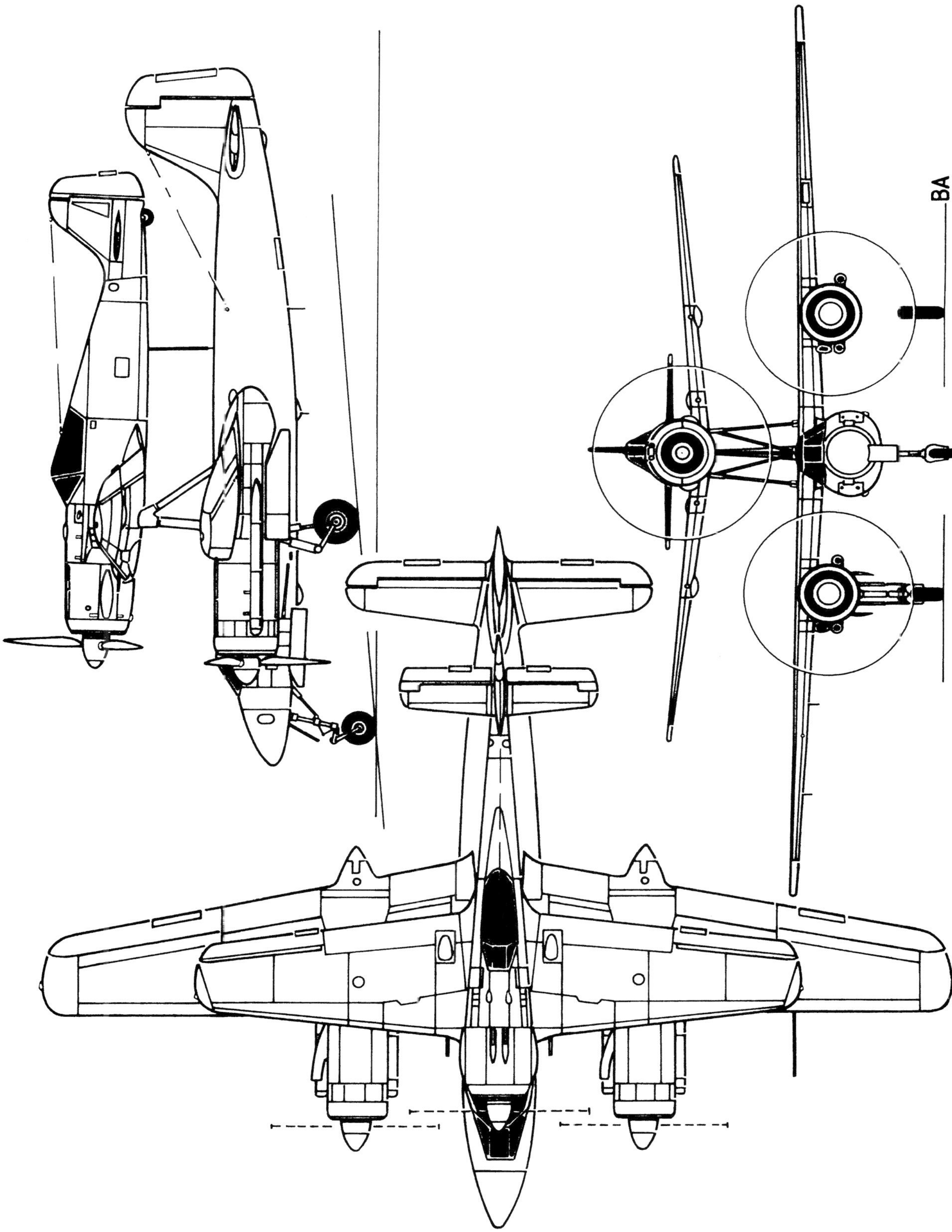

Three-view drawing of a Ta 154/Fw 190 A-8 Mistel combination (Beethoven device).

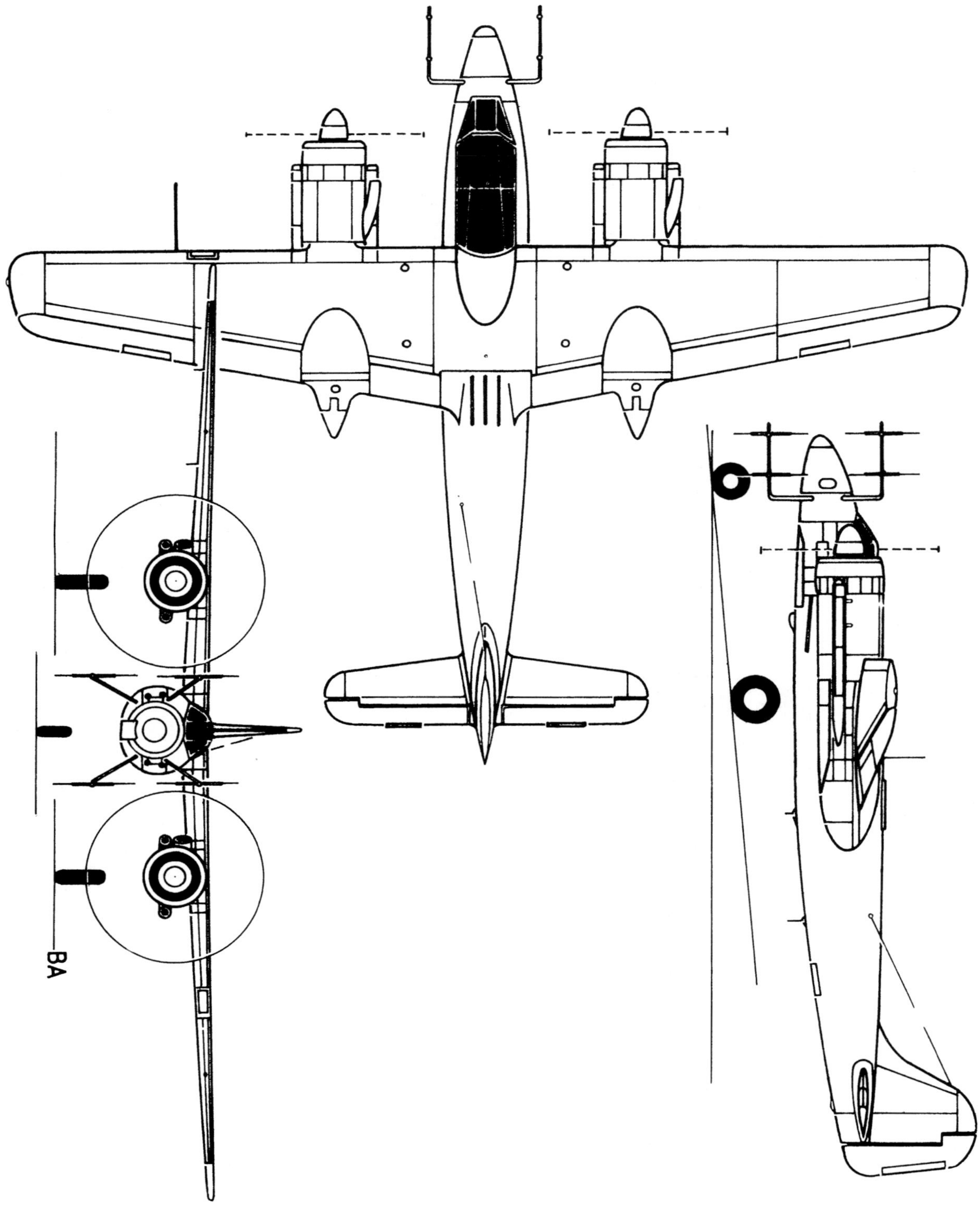

Three-view drawing of WerkNr. 120005 (TQ+XE).

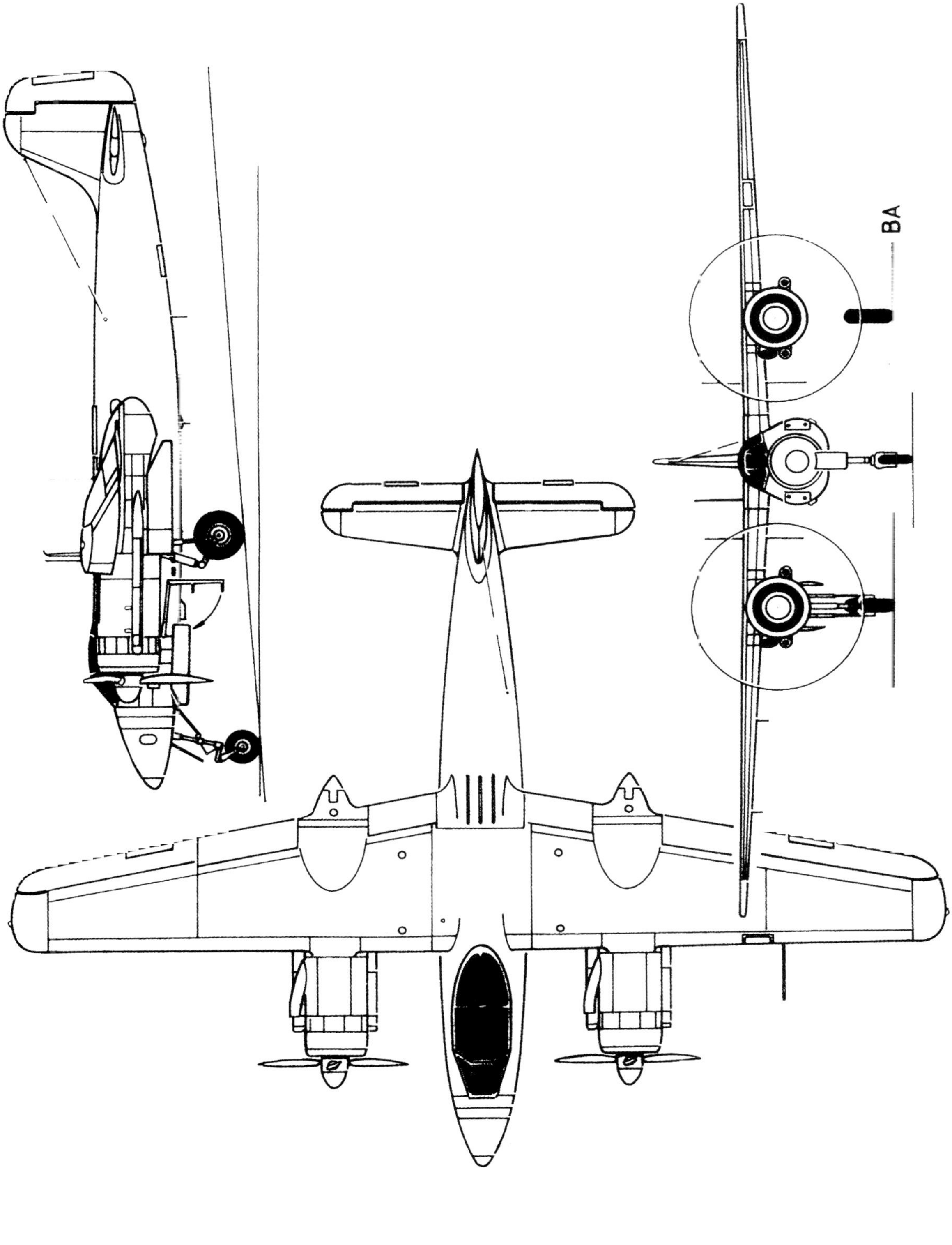

Three-view drawing of operational Ta 154 with radar antennas in wing center-section.

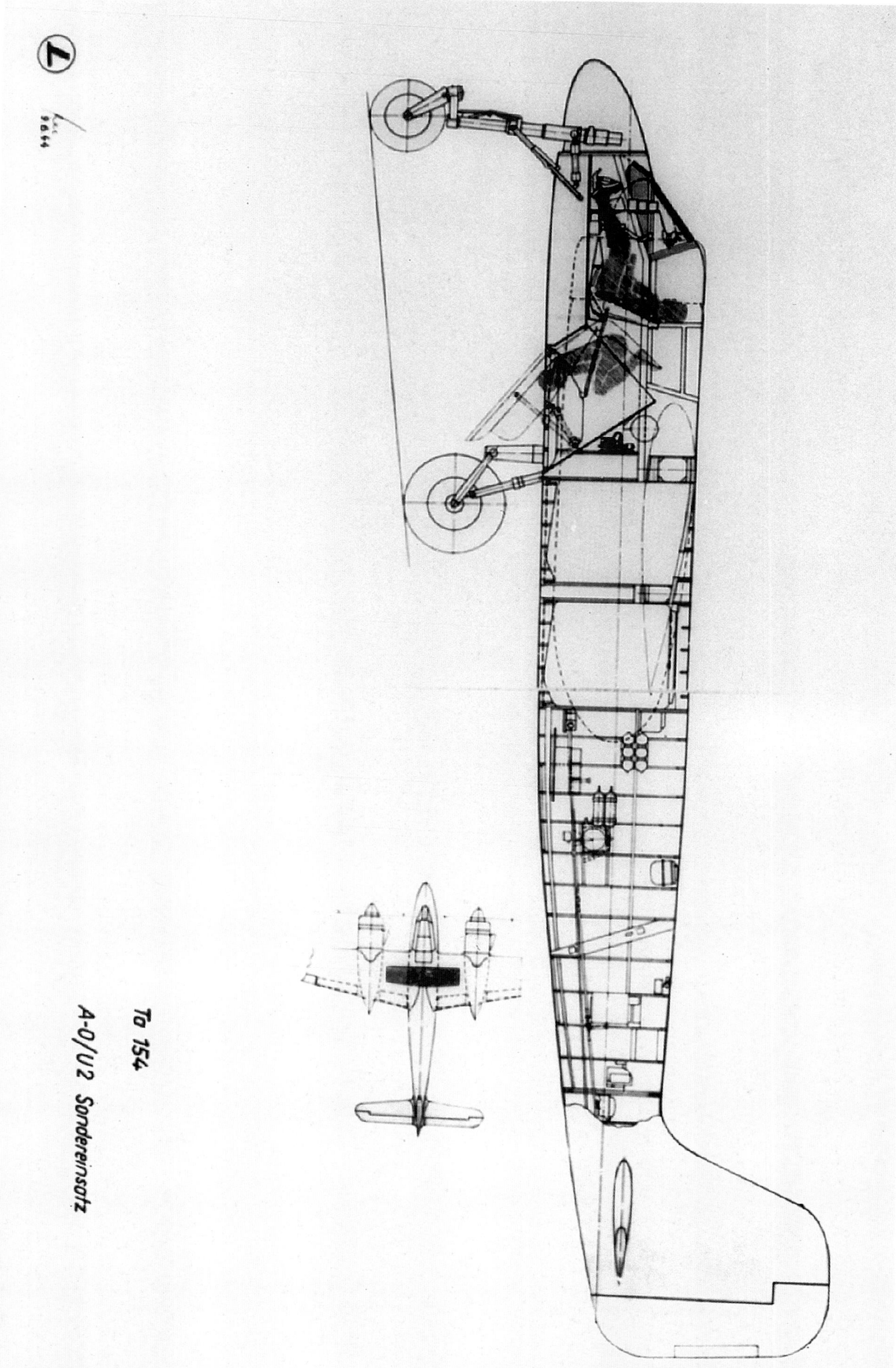
Ta 154
A-0/U2 Sondereinsatz

Ta 154

Type	WerkNr.	First mention	Fate/Last mention
Ta 154 V1	100001	01/07/1943	destroyed in air attack 05/08/1944
Ta 154 V2	100002	10/09/1943	destroyed in air attack 05/08/1944
Ta 154 V3	100003	25/11/1943	destroyed in air attack 05/08/1944
Ta 154 V4	100004	19/01/1944	destroyed in accident 20/06/1944
Ta 154 V5	100005	25/02/1944	converted to night fighter 14/08/1944
Ta 154 V6	100006	18/03/1944	converted to night fighter 27/09/1944
Ta 154 V7	100007	25/03/1944	destroyed in air attack 05/08/1944
Ta 154 V8	100008	08/04/1944	destroyed in crash landing 06/05/1944
Ta 154 V9	100009	18/04/1944	destroyed in crash landing 18/04/1944
Ta 154 V10	100010	04/06/1944	18/07/1944 unserviceable, engine trouble
Ta 154 V22	120001	12/06/1944	destroyed in air attack 05/08/1944
Ta 154 A-0	120002	16/04/1944	destroyed in air attack 05/08/1944
Ta 154 V23	120003	14/07/1944	ferried to Detmold on 12/08/1944
Ta 154 A-0	120004	25/05/1944	destroyed in air attack 05/08/1944
Ta 154 A-0	120005	30/06/1944	flight movement Langenhagen 19/11/1944
Ta 154 A-0	120006	not known	destroyed in air attack 05/08/1944
Ta 154 A-0	120007	—	construction by MMW Erfurt not certain
Ta 154 A-0	120008	—	construction by MMW Erfurt not certain
Ta 154 A-0	120009	not known	destroyed in air attack 05/08/1944
Ta 154 A-0	120010	—	construction not certain
Ta 154 A-0/U1	120011	—	construction not certain
Ta 154 A-0/U1	120012	—	construction not certain
Ta 154 A-0/U1	120013	—	construction not certain
Ta 154 A-0/U1	120014	July 1944	flight movement Langenhagen 01/07/1944
Ta 154 A-0/U1	120015	July 1944	blown up by NJG 3 April 1945
Ta 154 A-0/U1	120056	—	construction not certain
Ta 154 A-0/U1	120057	—	construction not certain
Ta 154 A-0/U1	120058	—	construction not certain
Ta 154 A-0/U1	120059	—	construction not certain
Ta 154 A-0/U1	120060	—	construction not certain
Ta 154 A-0/U1	120101	—	construction not certain
Ta 154 A-0/U1	120102	—	construction not certain
Ta 154 A-0/U1	120103	—	construction not certain
Ta 154 A-0/U1	120104	—	construction not certain
Ta 154 C-1	120105	—	aircraft not completed
Ta 154 C-2	120106	—	aircraft not completed
Ta 154 A-1	320002	12/06/1944	destroyed in crash 28/06/1944
Ta 154 A-1	320003	30/06/1944	with III/JG 2 in Lechfeld 15/04/1944
Ta 154 A-1	320004	June 1944	destroyed in crash landing 16/06/1944
Ta 154 A-1	320005	—	construction not certain
Ta 154 A-1	320006	06/07/1944	fate after August 1944 not known
Ta 154 A-1	320007	July 1944	damaged in crash 28/07/1944
Ta 154 A-2	320008	01/08/1944	damaged in belly landing 30/04/1944
Ta 154 A-2	320009	01/08/1944	blown up by NJG 3 April 1945
Ta 154 A-2	320010	01/08/1944	blown up by NJG 3 April 1945
Ta 154 A-2	320011	28/08/1944	destroyed in crash landing 28/09/1944
Ta 154 A-2	320012	—	completion not certain
Ta 154 A-2	320013	—	completion not certain
Ta 154 A-2	320014	—	completion not certain
Ta 154 A-2	320015	—	completion not certain
Ta 154 A-2	320016	—	completion not certain
Ta 154 A-2	320017	July 1944	parked at Kölleda airfield 01/08/1944
Ta 154 A-2	320018	—	construction not certain
Ta 154 A-2	320059	not known	parked at Langenhagen 30/10/1944

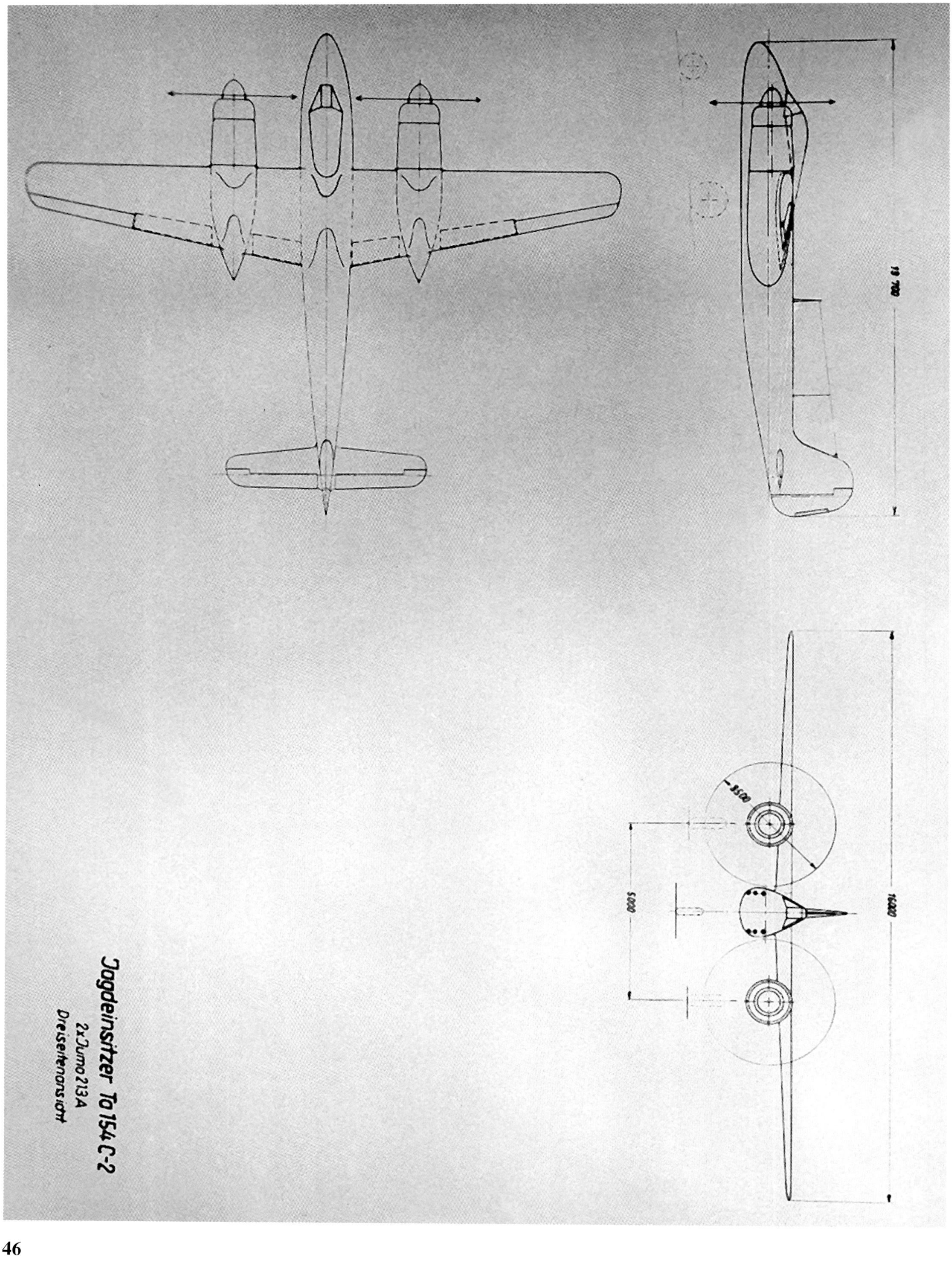
Jagdeinsitzer Ta 154 C-2
2x Jumo 213A
Dreiseitenansicht
3500
5000
16 000

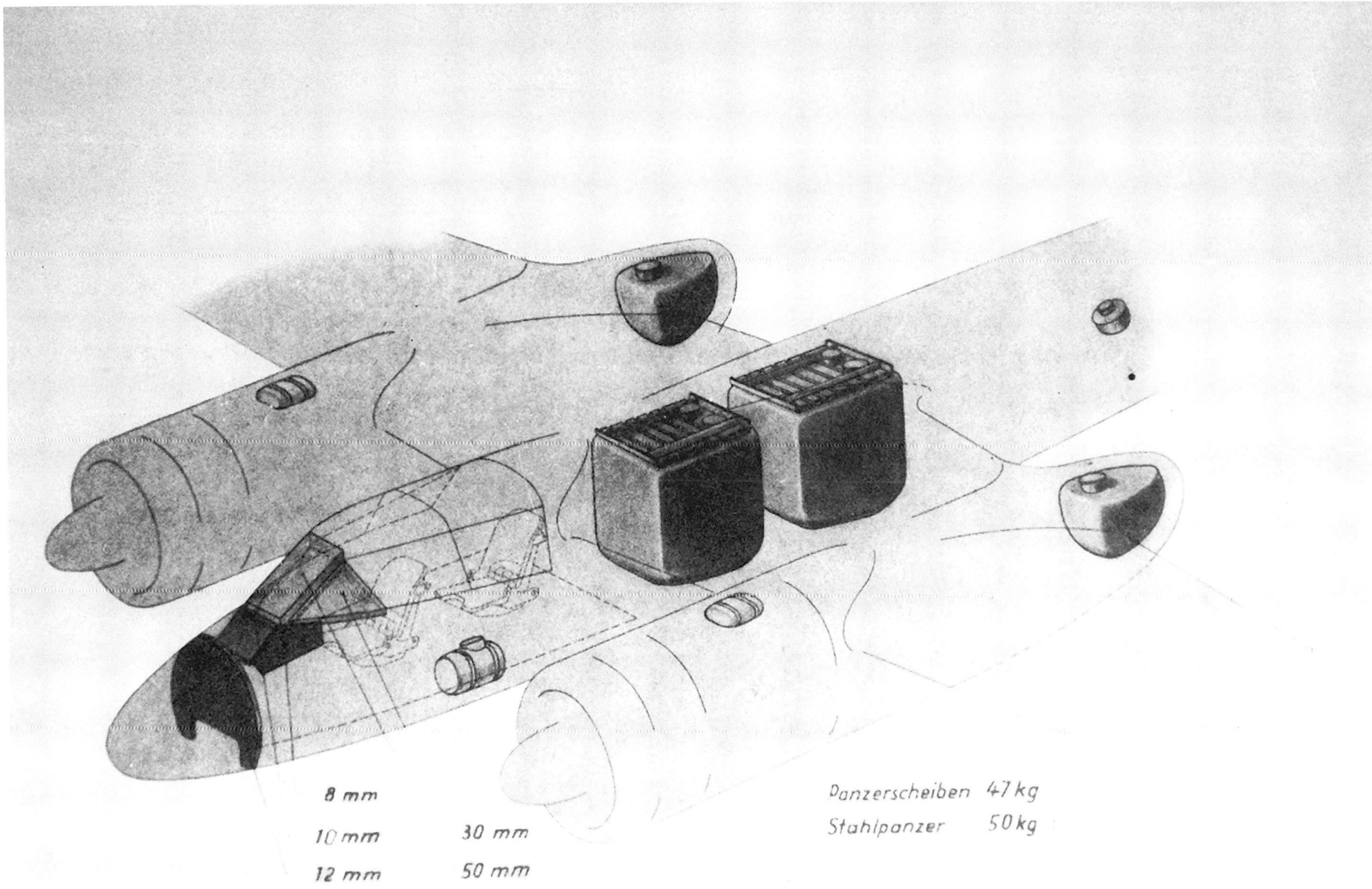

Nachtjäger Ta 154
Behälteranlage u. Panzerung

Ta 154 A-2/U4 of Stab III/NJG 3 with the registration D5 + HD, seen here following its crash landing. Note the wing-mounted antennas.

Side view of the crashed machine.

Crash of an operational Ta 154 A-2/U4

An RAF pilot inspects the wreck. The photo provides a look at the radio operator's position.